IT ALL STARTS WITH YOU!

Published by Brolga Publishing Pty Ltd
ABN 46 063 962 443
PO Box 12544, A'Beckett St, Melbourne, VIC, 8006, Australia
email: admin@brolgapublishing.com.au

Copyright © Kevin O'Reilly 2009

All rights reserved. No part of this publication may be reproduced, stored in a retrieval system, or transmitted in any form or by any means, electronic, mechanical, photocopying, recording or otherwise, without the prior permission of the Publisher.

National Library of Australia Cataloguing-in-Publication entry

        O'Reilly, Kevin Sherwood, 1966-
        It all starts with you! : unlock the power of your full potential
        9781921596001 (pbk.)
        Self-actualisation (Psychology)
        Self-realisation.
        Success.
        158.1

Printed in China
Cover design by David Khan
Typeset and design by Imogen Stubbs

IT ALL STARTS WITH
YOU!

Unlock The Power Of Your Full Potential

KEVIN O'REILLY

It all starts with you! is a "self-help" and "personal development" book designed to give the reader insight into the many wonderful "laws of the universe" that the author has successfully used to achieve not only personal goals, but to achieve true happiness and "joyful living".

This book is indeed a journey of self discovery, and offers a clear and logical explanation for the reason why the majority of people fail to realise their full and unlimited human potential.

In Memory of William (Bill) O'Reilly (1939 – 2001)
To whom I dedicate this book.

Contents

1	It all starts with you	1
2	Looking at life through the rear vision mirror	19
3	The universal law of vibration and attraction	27
4	Visualisation to develop goal setting	59
5	Empathy	77
6	Passion for what it is you do	87
7	I.Q. vs E.Q.	95
8	Spirituality	105
9	Your health is your wealth	121
10	Application	129

1 **It all starts with you.** Looks at what I call accountability, in that we must all take responsibility for our own actions. Playing the blame game is a negative and very limiting process. Personal growth and development can only occur when you have a full and complete understanding of this basic concept.

2 **Looking at life through the rear vision mirror.** Introduces us to the concept that the results that you have achieved up till now are the product of our thoughts, and begins to show how through "right thinking" and "goal setting", future results need not be dictated by past performance.

3 **The universal law of vibration and attraction.** Explores the link between the attraction to things we are in harmony with. The law of attraction when correctly understood allows us to achieve the things we most think about, as we truly become what we think about the most. Our thoughts become our feelings and our feelings determine our actions. This chapter will undoubtably seem quite foreign to the uninitiated, as the ideas contained in this chapter will really stretch your understanding in the field of vibration and energy.

4 **Visualisation to develop goal setting.** Goal setting is such a misunderstood and under-utilised idea, yet has the potential to allow you to achieve your wildest dreams. Visualisation when used in conjunction with goal setting provides the link between feelings and when you involve your feelings your ideas become far more potent, with a high probability of actually achieving your goal. It's what separates goal setting from simply wishful thinking.

5 **Empathy.** What a beautiful word, the ability to have empathy for someone else and their current circumstance is such a fundamental element in the art of communication. In this chapter we look at improving your communication skills, by simply having empathy for what it is the person you are talking to is saying and what it means to you, not the ability to recall information word for word. Empathy leads to the fundamental understanding of higher learning and education. When the ideas contained within this chapter are correctly applied, a whole new world of education and application of knowledge is unlocked.

6 **Passion for what it is you do.** In this chapter we look at just what it is within us, that driving force of motivation from deep within, and how to develop and use this emotion towards what we desire, truly a powerful concept when fully understood. Closely linked to empathy, however, passion comes from within. This chapter will help the reader better understand their innermost thoughts, their "Sanctum Sanctorum" the me that I see is the me I will be. We look at your self image and how to improve it by gaining an understanding of yourself.

7 I.Q. vs E.Q. In this chapter we look at the relationship between I.Q. (Intelligence Quota) and E.Q. (Emotional Quota) or emotional intelligence. By applying all of the ideas from the previous chapters we learn how to stretch and grow from our own life experiences, face our fears and become a better, stronger person by doing so.

8 Spirituality. A holistic look at one's self, understanding the three key elements in our own life so they will all be in harmony, focusing on creating happiness in your own life.

9 Your health is your wealth. Following on from the previous chapter, we look at our physical body and how to improve the efficiency of the body, in order to get more out of it and to maximise our life expectancy.

10 Application. By applying everything we have discussed to your life and the pursuit of happiness. Trying everything that you have read in this book and applying it to your own life and circumstances, and applying this knowledge to achieve the elusive pursuit of happiness. By making the right choices and holding onto your beliefs, goals and desires you can and will improve the quality of your life, and after all, that is what life is all about, building a rich and happy life or as I like to call it "building a legacy".

INTRODUCTION

KEVIN O'REILLY: born in Brisbane, Australia in 1966, youngest of three children, I grew up with a fairly normal childhood; however, from a very early age it was apparent to me that my father was anything but average. I remember him as a very strong-willed and successful leader in the business sector. In my teenage years, I can recall watching him in action at his work. I was amazed by his ability to **communicate** with his staff, and observed the respect from his staff it seemed to bring. In my own business career, I am thankful that this is one attribute that I seemed to have inherited.

Due to my father's focus on his career, we relocated to Adelaide, South Australia in the mid 1980s. After a fairly shaky transition from the Queensland education system to the South Australian education system, I was quite keen to move on and leave school in my matriculation year and look for employment. It was at this point that perhaps the most defining event occurred. Good fortune smiled on me and I very quickly landed an apprenticeship as a refrigeration mechanic. Finally, I had something that seemed to make sense to me. All my life I have been a tactile person, struggling with academia, with my apprenticeship I was able to flourish.

In my working career, I have been fortunate to try several aspects of the air-conditioning industry, from specialised commissioning in multi-story commercial buildings, to equipment sales, evolving into consulting and leading to my current position of director and a major shareholder of System Solutions Engineering Pty Ltd.

At the time of writing this, I am also on the Board of Directors of AIRAH (the Australian Institute of Refrigeration and Air-conditioning and Heating) which is a "not for profit" industry body, who's primary role is to provide education to its members, and to provide a voice for the industry. AIRAH has also been called upon to provide advice to the Government in matters relating to the environmental issues such as global warming energy consumption and impact on the environment from air-conditioning systems, to ozone depletion resulting from refrigerants and the like.

In both of my roles as a director, and with over twenty-five years in the refrigeration and air conditioning industry, it has become abundantly clear to me that leadership is earned from **leading by example**, not by force (that's a dictatorship). You quickly earn the respect of your peers and employees when you lead by example, have empathy for their situation and work as a team.

So what was the motivation for me to write this book? Well it's quite simple. Over the past few years, I found myself performing a significant amount of public speaking, and it seemed the more speaking that I did, the more I enjoyed doing it (more about this point in the chapter *I.Q. vs E.Q.*), eventually leading to an invitation to speak at the Regency Park TAFE graduation dinner in front of 350 people (my largest audience at that time). I was given the opportunity to talk about my time as an apprentice some twenty-three years earlier, and my journey to become a company director and industry leader. Naturally, I used this opportunity to talk about emotional intelligence and goal setting, and a very basic overview of the ideas contained in this book.

In the following months, I found myself talking about it to staff in a counselling capacity or fellow industry people or friends about my beliefs on the topics contained in this book. It occupied so much of my thought process, but each time I spoke about one of these topics, I found my own understanding of the subject matter increased, becoming more defined and refined. So I had the revelation/idea to put my thoughts and beliefs into this book. This would give me the opportunity to go back and review the comments, stories and develop my own understanding of the many ideas contained within this book.

It is my wish that the information and ideas in this book can be used by the reader to help gain an understanding of what I call the "laws of the universe" as they have helped me and those around me gain happiness and understanding in the journey of life. As I have always said, ignorance is overcome by education and awareness, so join me now in a journey of awareness and self discovery, as together we unlock your full potential as you take your first step into a much bigger world. Enjoy the ride and I hope you can use the ideas in this book and put them to good use. As the great Asian philosopher Confucius said: **every journey starts with the very first step.**

1 IT ALL STARTS WITH YOU

It is a well documented fact that a great majority of people do not achieve anywhere near their full potential, and if they were to be asked why that is the case, their explanation would be simply this: "Nobody has done it for me" or "It's not my fault" or even "Don't blame me... It's too hard", etc.

What they are really saying is, I don't know how to change my life, all I have now is all I want, I am comfortable with my life, why should I change? When in reality this mind set is called the "comfort zone" and it's a bad place to be. You see, the comfort zone is simply poor conditioning throughout our life, allowing habit to run our life and choosing to live life on the path of least resistance.

It starts when our parents say, Johnnie, don't do this and don't do that, or you can't possibly have a car or a house like that, because I don't, you should settle for this much more affordable car or this cheaper house. This continuous **conditioning** becomes imbedded in our programming, and before long it is all we know. We go through life with somebody else's ideals and expectations, when only those who dare to dream to be different and who manage to hold onto their individuality become the exception and are labelled a "non-conformist" and are judged by a critical society.

Eventually we get through the school years, where after twelve or so years we have either become a conformist or a rebel, where our teachers are glad to see the end of us. However, in my opinion the schooling system (or at least twenty plus years ago when I was a student) is not set up properly to train students for life. Once we leave the relative safety net of school and are thrust into the working world, we develop a **sink** or **swim** approach, and in most cases we just get buy, struggling to pay our bills and to put food on the table. Not a very rosy picture is it? But unfortunately this scenario represents the majority of people and how the events of life dictate our outcome. We lack the proper training to do much about it, eventually our pride and **habitual thinking** trap us in this mindset that is called the comfort zone.

At this point, I want you to realise that this **old conditioning** is simply old programming and if you want more out of life, you simply need to understand one very important point. The point is that you can have, say, be and achieve anything your mind can conceive. It is critical at this juncture to understand the topic of this chapter and that is, **It all starts with you.** If you can get past the blame game and take responsibility for your results in your life up to this point, then you have mastered the first step, and don't worry as the following chapters will show you the way to move forward.

If, however, you are struggling with this concept and your thoughts dwell on fear of upsetting your elders or parents or you feel intimidated by your peers, well it is clear you need to read on and re-read this chapter a few times as you have not yet grasped the point of this chapter. By simply glossing or skimming over the content to follow you will not gain the understanding of the topic that is required, it is the awareness and understanding of our self that is required in order to define who we are and accept what we have done up to this point. That does not mean that we are now all we will ever be, it simply means that the results and outcome is not what we wanted, or we have fallen short of our original goals, but that's okay, at least we know. It is this ability to identify that short coming and build on it, which is where we will focus.

> **"Most human limitations are self imposed."**
>
> Denis Waitley

Let me digress: at this point I should tell the story about my introduction to the ideas and concepts I am talking about.

The Tony Keynes story:

I had been working for some time in the air-conditioning industry as an apprentice refrigeration mechanic, then as a tradesman for one of the largest mechanical service contractors in South Australia at that time, a company called Butterfields S.A. I had left my career as a tradesman and was developing my career in sales. This career move was brought about by someone who would become a great mentor and friend of mine, the first of many mentors (outside of my family that is) and his name was Tony Keynes. I remember the event when I made the transition from a tradesman, working on building sites in and around the city of Adelaide. By this time, I had been quite successful in the industry as it all seemed to make sense to me. After working on new buildings, my role was to "commission" the newly installed air-conditioning plant. This simply involved running the new equipment and ensuring it performed to the designed specification. Once the equipment was running correctly we would prove the operation to the designing consultants and during the handover period it was my role to instruct the new occupants of the facility how to safely operate the air-conditioning system. It was during the finishing periods of a multi-storey building in the city when Tony, who was a supplier in the industry, approached me and over the course of a lunch, suggested that I had an ability to communicate and that, combined with my technical knowledge, meant that I would make a great **salesman**. Imagine me as a salesman, when all I had known up to that point was being a tradesman.

I can recall the feelings of doubt at that time. The fear was overwhelming. What if I was to leave my trusted and respected career, what if… what if… Fear was holding me back. My first memory of the **comfort zone** was being played out. Fortunately, for me Tony was a great salesman, and he convinced me that he needed assistance in the sales field as he had won a multi-million dollar project and lacked the technical expertise to guarantee the satisfactory delivery of this prestigious project.

Now Tony was not your ordinary salesmen, he was a real "goal setter", a very inspired man, an athletic person who gave back to little athletics as much as he did to the industry. But for me the real breakthrough was in Tony's belief in personal training and personal development. It was not long before I attended my first weekend sales and motivation seminar. I will never forget it. The programme was called **"Born Rich"** and it was delivered by a man who was to become my second mentor, a great teacher and philosopher called Bob Proctor.

I cannot begin to describe just how powerful the ideas were that unfolded over the course of the weekend, other than to say it was life changing. I was immediately able to apply some of the ideas in my new-found sales career, but it was longer term that the ideas became imbedded in my psyche. You see it was not so much the immediate knowledge that I had been exposed to, but the ongoing education and **habit breaking** concepts that I felt made the difference. For example, as a part of the training package we were given an audio copy of the seminar. This was in the form of eight audio cassettes, yes remember cassettes? I would play them over and over until the subject matter was deeply imbedded in my being, and the tapes actually wore out. I found myself recalling information in conversations with people, but what I was actually doing was recalling **what it meant to me** – big difference. I will discuss more about this topic in the following chapters.

I encourage you to search for yourself this wonderful educational experience. Just do a search on "Bob Proctor seminars" on the internet and follow the links, as I can not possibly do justice to this life changing experience. Not a day goes by when I do not use at least one of the elements and ideas, and that is what it is all about, by gaining an increased awareness from exposure to new ideas, and really making us **think**, setting us free from our "old habitual self".

Needless to say, both Tony and I were able to achieve some amazing results in the sales field. By applying the goal setting techniques we learnt that old conditional thinking could be changed, and I still apply this philosophy to this day.

The next step for me was to take these ideas and to apply them to my private and personal life. I had been harbouring a desire to stretch out and do exactly what I was doing with Tony, but to do it for myself. I will never forget the exact scene, we were both attending yet another weekend seminar (also by Bob Proctor) when it suddenly hit me, I could have what I wanted. My goal at that time was to start my own business, as this allowed me to work from home as my children were at that time very young, and it was important to me to spend as much time in their young lives. I can recall turning to Tony with a big smile on my face and saying, "Tony you may not like what I am about to tell you, but I have a goal, and I want you to help me achieve it."

Needless to say, Tony could see where my motivation was coming from, and because he had been exposed to the same **right thinking** and goal setting information that I had, he was actually quite supportive, and before long, I had achieved exactly what I wanted, selling the same equipment I had been selling, but doing it for myself.

That was fifteen years ago. Let me now tell you a story that unfolded in my life not so long ago.

I can understand if you are thinking that my life has been a bed of roses, that I have achieved everything that I have desired. Well let me assure you that nothing could be further from the truth.

Perhaps one of my greatest disappointments has been the failure of my marriage. Like so many couples in today's society, my wife and I had become very different people after eighteen years of marriage. And like thousands of men in a similar situation I had become quite comfortable in what had become a "loveless marriage". Now I am not saying that there was never love there, in fact I can recall a time when my wife and I truly did love each other; however, as time went by we became different people, and we became more house mates rather than soul mates. I will never forget the day that my wife came to me and said that she wanted to leave, as she put it, so we may each find the love that we truly deserve. This idea seemed completely foreign to me at that time, but now with the benefit of four years hindsight and the love of two women since, I can see what her motivation was.

I have now also come to understand that after such a long period of time, change in each other must be expected, so the trick is not to see this as a failure but realise the changes that make us each individuals will in turn lead towards a change in "attraction" to each other. I will define this point much later, when we discuss the laws of vibration and attraction.

The interesting point that I want to make is that even in my darkest hour, I made the conscious choice (and that is exactly what it was, a choice) to work towards a successful separation. Some of my friends had just been through a very messy and difficult separation, ending up in the courts and both parties making it as difficult for each other as humanly possible. I saw first hand the resentment and hurt this caused, when in reality neither side was victorious, and often the children were the ones who were caught up in the middle of all this negativity.

At this point I feel it necessary to quote one of my favourite sayings, **"It's not who we are underneath, but what we do that defines us"** and it is this saying that I feel best describes the essence of this chapter. It does not matter of what riches or poverty or circumstance we are born into, what matters is what we do in the face of adversity. The decisions we make truly define us, whether we have empathy for somebody or whether we find it easier to look away and not lend a helping hand, these are the very things that define us. In my opinion, it is as simple as the **choices we make.** I mention this particular circumstance as it highlights two ways to look at one event. You see I could choose to look at my separation and ensuing divorce as a dismal failure and let the associated negativity creep into my life or choose to look at it for what it was, a happy and successful time when we were together, from which three beautiful children are living their own lives. I can honestly say now that I do not harbour any ill feeling towards my ex, as a matter of fact we enjoy quite a close relationship.

This has also flowed onto our children. Children are very perceptive, they can sense when there is tension between their parents. In far too many cases, one or both of the parents attempt to poison their young minds towards the mother or father in an attempt to satisfy their own resentment or ill-feeling. What a mixed up and crazy perspective must exist in the mind of these poor and unfortunate people who do not understand that it is them and only them who is responsible for their lot in life.

When you understand that, you realise everything that you have in your life is a direct result of your choices.

In the following chapters I will further define this point; that your choices are simply the result of your **thoughts**. In this chapter the focus is to understand the concept of "accountability". You must believe that you are accountable for your actions. You cannot blame anyone else.

Enough said about that chapter of my life, I raised it to make a further point. The point is that I had allowed the circumstances in my life at that time (and for some time before these events) when I had actually forgotten to implement and use the many aspects of goal setting and other powerful laws that I have deliberately not devolved to you at this time. There was a time when I was living in the comfort zone and just getting by, but I made the profound realisation that I was indeed lost, and my life could be so much more.

I was talking to a friend and employee of mine, Marc. Marc and I would often have profound conversations about the state of the environment and global warming, a topic that I was gaining more and more understanding of due to my association as a consultant in the building services industry. However, Marc and I were talking about a recent movie that had been promoted called *The Secret*. Neither one of us had seen this movie or knew much about *The Secret* at that time so as Marc was into computers (he was a CAD drafter) he decided to Google search this topic. To my amazement a familiar name popped up, and that was of course Bob Proctor. After reading the blurb about *The Secret* I turned to Marc and proclaimed "I can't believe it, I know the secret", I had just forgotten it.

All of a sudden, as if a switch had been turned on, I could recall the countless hours of tapes I had listened to years before. Naturally, I purchased my own copy of the DVD and after watching it several times, I bought the book. The impact that this book and DVD would have on me was amazing, I can only describe it to be as profound as the original Bob Proctor seminars some fifteen years earlier.

Once again, I will stress that I cannot possibly highlight the wonderful messages of life that are contained within *The Secret*, other than to say that I completely recommend that you source a copy for yourself and watch it several times over. I am convinced that many of the points that I talk about in this book are well documented in *The Secret*. The fundamental difference is that I have tried to talk about my life experiences and events that are unique to me, in the hope that you may be able to take some of these ideas and bring clarity and meaning to your life. Such is the nature of these ideals and philosophies that no one can take credit for them, they have been around for centuries, it is just that nobody talks about it or it may not be fashionable to talk about human potential. What a waste of knowledge. This is a situation that I am keen to rectify, one that I see is critical when understanding the true human potential that is our fundamental birthright.

To bring further clarity to the topic of responsibility and accountability, think about the professional sportsperson. It does not matter what particular sport you think of, for no matter what sport you look at the person who is excelling in that particular sport completely understands the essence of this chapter. Their results are directly related to their input, focus, passion and determination.

If the sport involves physical fitness like cycling or running for example, the athlete knows that he or she must **practise** their profession. Remember, the term professional just means that you derive an income from what it is you do. A professional sportsperson may have no other form of income, relying only on sponsorship or prize money to survive. Clearly if they excel in their sport the financial rewards will be much greater, take Tiger Woods for example.

My point here is simply this: in sport and in life, the more you practise, focus and concentrate on the goal or task at hand, the more chance you will have in succeeding. In cycling for example, fitness is paramount, but fitness is achieved by hours and hours of training. The cyclist knows that nobody else can do this training for them. Both body and mind has been conditioned to race the clock, or other competitors, and when each of the other competitors has the same understanding you have the basis for a great race.

As you can see, it does not matter what sport you look at, physical fitness is only achieved by physically pushing your boundaries, by endless hours of exertion. Imagine if the athlete did not want to be there and was not motivated, how successful do you think they would be? I have tremendous respect for professional athletes and sports-people as they demonstrate the essence of these principals of accountability and responsibility and their results are clearly measurable.

> **"Pain is temporary. It may last a minute, or an hour, or a day, or a year, but eventually it will subside and something else will take its place. If I quit, however, it lasts forever."**
>
> Lance Armstrong

One final area that I want to mention and no doubt some will take offence to this delicate subject, but I raise the topic as it further defines the principals of this chapter. And that is our physical image. The person you see when you look into the mirror.

What better way to close this chapter than to talk about you and the physical body? Are you happy with the way you look? By now you should be able to grasp the point that your body and your appearance is a direct result of the understanding of this chapter. Do you blame everyone else around you for the way you look? (I am talking generally about your weight and fitness here, not if you are injured in some way).

Your physical appearance is a direct result of your inner picture of you, the self image, and we will discuss self image in a later chapter. However, I want to focus on happiness with one's appearance, or lack of it. So many people complain about being overweight, they spend a fortune on weight loss products, and try all sorts of fad diets, without success. But unless you understand the link between taking responsibility for your own actions, and develop a clean and healthy lifestyle and healthy self image you are wasting your time.

In my years of reading health magazines and developing my own fitness program, I can assure you our body's respond to one simple equation: kilojoules (food intake) must be balanced, or if weight loss is desired less than kilojoules of output. It is as simple as that. If you do not burn off the calories of food that you ingest, you will store this excess as body fat. Combine this with today's lifestyle, where childhood obesity and the reported cases of diabetes are on the increase. It is all related!

We must remain active. With all of the modern conveniences like cars and buses around today, we are losing the basis of movement and motion in general, and society is becoming lazy. But when you understand this point then you can make a change and do something about it. Become more active, walk, run, ride a bike, it really does not matter what you do to raise your heart rate, what is important is that you exercise regularly, three or more times a week and understand the relationship between the food that you put into your mouth and the consequence to your waist line.

If you fall into this category, use the information in this book to help you to build a healthy self image. When you get that part right you are on the path to developing a healthy body by implementing a healthy lifestyle. But you must get your mind and self image right first before you go any further.

This is something that I have personal experience with. I previously mentioned that there was a time a few years ago when I had allowed complacency to run my life. I had forgotten this most basic point, I was eating more then I was expelling in energy output. Naturally, weight gain (or fat gain/storage as I call it) was occurring. I am not talking morbid obesity here, I would consider it more like an unhealthy state, and more importantly, I was not happy with what I saw when I looked into the mirror.

Initially, I found it quite difficult to lose weight. I had started exercising, but that only slowed the gain, I was not actually losing weight. Eventually, I realised that I was eating too much. You see the older you get the slower your metabolism gets and the less you can eat without putting on weight. Only after reading various health magazines did I learn just how delicate a balance food intake and physical activity was. In order to lose fat, I had to eat healthy and increase activity. The more exercise I did the more I enjoyed it, and one of the most important truths that is the essence of this book was revealed, that is if you truly enjoy what you do, you become very good at it. This is true for our career and activity, sporting and lifestyle. Eventually I developed a programme that was both sustainable and enjoyable and the result was that I achieved my goal. Not only did I lose body fat, but when I look in the mirror, I see the physical image that I expect of myself. This in turn brings a tremendous amount of satisfaction and pride to my life.

I want to mention one final point about physical self image and the power of our mind. Now I have achieved what I consider to be the physical manifestation of my self image, I witness something that is quite unexpected, and that is the power of the subconscious mind. Anytime you eat something that is not so healthy, our subconscious mind kicks in and you think something along the lines of: if you eat this, you know how many kilometres on the exercise bike you will need to ride to burn of the calories contained in that food stuff. On the other hand, if you are feeling a bit flat, and could not be bothered to exercise today, your subconscious mind kicks in again and you think something along the lines of: if you don't exercise today, then you will not have performed enough physical activity to offset your food intake. Keep this up and you will become a "fatty-boom-bah".

You see the power of the subconscious mind, through conditioning and training which is done by performing (in this case) healthy choices for a prolonged period of time. We build a new habit and that is how it works. What we do for the majority of time is truly who we are. If you don't like who you are, you can change it. The following chapters will provide further clarity to this very point. Understanding and awareness will always overcome ignorance.

> **"Lack of activity destroys the good condition of every human being, while movement and methodical physical exercise save and preserve it."**
>
> *Plato*

2 LOOKING AT LIFE THROUGH THE REAR VISION MIRROR

Unusual name for a chapter, I know, however it is simply a comparative description for a **state of mind**. When you look into the rear vision mirror of your car while driving in a forward direction, all you see is the immediate past, and to continue with this mind set in place all you will achieve is **more of the same**.

I actually think this saying has two meanings. The first and most obvious relates to observing the past and seeing only the results of your journey so far, with distant objects that were past some time ago fading into the distance and out of sight.

There is a second and less obvious ideal within this concept, and that is: if you are driving your car on a freeway at say 100km per hour, and you are only looking into the rear vision mirror, how long will it be before you crash? Profound when you think about it, but life is truly like this. If you do not spend the majority of time looking forward and planning your journey, avoiding the unforeseen obstacles, and making changes in direction when the road requires us to do so, you will not complete your intended journey.

The comparison is simply this, how many of us actually live our life, using the results of the past to determine our future outcome? I believe the great majority of people do this (myself included, until I fully understood this concept). Not only with regards to results but following on from the previous chapter, where we looked at taking responsibility for your own results and actions. With a thorough understanding of this concept, you will develop the awareness that you, and only you, control your **journey through life**. This is a powerful concept, yes you are in charge of your destiny, and don't let anyone tell you otherwise.

Repeat this idea in your mind over and over a few times, understand the relationship between this phrase and the journey of life. You are in the driver's seat and you may be fortunate to have a navigator sitting next to you helping you by providing guidance, but for the most part, you are on your own, you control the speed, the path which in turn controls your direction, resulting in reaching your destination; your goals.

> **"It isn't what you have or who you are or where you are or what you are doing that makes you happy or unhappy. It is what you think about."**
>
> *Dale Carnegie*

Marc's story:

I have previously talked about Marc and the profound conversations we used to have about all manner of items, however, I think this story really captures the essence of the chapter.

Marc and I had been to a job site one day, and on our return journey to the office we decided to drop into my apartment as it was on the way and Marc had not seen my "bach pad". After a quick coffee and a look around, we were driving on the freeway heading back to our office when Marc said to me, "You know you are so lucky, you have everything you want, nice apartment, Plasma TV, great job. How come I don't have everything that I want?" Wow, what a bombshell, but the interesting thing was that I said, "Marc I know exactly why you don't have all the things in your life that you desire, simply because you are living your life as if you are looking in the rear vision mirror." Now given that we were actually driving on the freeway at that instant, the analogy was easy to describe. I explained to Marc that because I knew him so well, I could clearly see that he lacked direction.

In previous conversations with Marc, he had told me about the various career paths he had chosen, and could not understand why he would change his mind so often and usually not complete what he had started. You see his whole life had been a succession of try this, don't like it, try that, too hard, do something else, etc. I said to him that with this current mind set, the results he was getting were consistent, and that unless he changed his thinking, he would only achieve more of the same thing.

Using myself as an example, I explained to Marc that I basically have been doing the same thing (or at least in the same industry) for the past twenty years so I should be good at it by now. You see what I do in my career comes very easily to me. Fundamentally, the mechanical services industry is based on very defined and scientific laws. This simply means that it is always repeatable and predictable, and with at that time twenty years of experience, I could now use my practical knowledge with my new found engineering knowledge and have a degree of confidence in what I was saying. And because I believed that was the case, I had very little trouble in convincing those around me or those I was consulting to.

The change in Marc that I was to observe in the next few weeks was amazing, he would spend hours on the internet searching out leaders and motivators, downloading podcasts and listening intently. You see Marc was looking for something, but still could not identify exactly what it was he was looking for. He was now on a journey of "spiritual enlightenment" and so far as I know he still is.

But perhaps the most important thing that I want to raise and is the real essence of this topic is that while he was listening to all of the educational material and I had witnessed his self image improve and his awareness in himself improve, he was still struggling with achieving personal happiness. He had established defined goals for establishing his new house, building the shed, planting trees and the like, but still was not truly happy.

One day I said to him, "Marc, you do not appear to be happy, what is wrong?" He said that now he knew how to **think** about happiness, he was quickly realising that what he was doing was not making him happy. For example the one hour drive to and from work each day was driving him mad. He also said that he was not deriving satisfaction in his job as a CAD drafter. Naturally I was disappointed to hear this as I truly enjoyed working with Marc, someone I could discuss environmental issues with and have the most profound deep and meaningful conversations. However, I asked Marc what exactly did he want and what would make him happy? He and his wife were thinking of moving to Tasmania, but did not believe that this was possible because of all the pressures and commitments.

To finish off this story as this is the final point I want to talk about, Marc was still indecisive about the move. We then talked about the perception of his commitments and pressures to stay versus the desire to move. It simply came down to making a decision. I said to Marc for everything we had talked about, with his new understanding of goal setting, self image and the like, it was as simple as deciding to go. So put your house on the market, unless you do this you will only get more of the same indecisiveness. He eventually became quite excited and truly believed that the move was possible, his wife and he had shared the same dream. Once they had made the decision to put their house on the market and sell, the rest seemed to fall into place. And I am pleased to say that my "tree hugging" friend Marc is doing exactly what he dreamt of doing, and that is to hug trees in Tasmania. (I know he won't mind me calling him a tree hugger, by his own description he is a passive environmentalist).

Now hopefully the true intent of this story is understood, that simply understanding the relationship between our results or outcome is determined by our thoughts, feelings and actions, not the other way around. Don't allow your circumstances or environment to determine your thoughts. Understand that we have control of our life by holding onto our beliefs and focusing on our goals, and we will delve much more

deeply into this concept in the following chapters.
This event also served to highlight the fact that we all are searching for different meaning, for example, what motivated Marc was not the same as my own motivations. The physical things, objects and possessions we attract into our lives are different for each of us, we are truly unique!

> **"To find yourself,
> think for yourself."**
>
> *Socrates*

3 THE UNIVERSAL LAW OF VIBRATION AND ATTRACTION

This is perhaps the most difficult chapter of this book to fully understand, and as I write these words I am wondering just how I can properly explain what is the most important concept of this whole book. Moreover, to explain a concept that for some strange reason is not taught to students or discussed around the water cooler at work. Yet understanding this universal and natural law has given me so much, it is my belief that this concept holds the key to unlocking the unlimited potential of our mind, it holds the key to achieving literally anything you want.

So if you are reading these words for the first time, or if you have not developed an understanding of the law of vibration and attraction, you may find the following chapter stretches your boundaries. In reality that is the definition of learning: to be exposed to a new idea or concept. I must admit, I was first introduced to this very concept some fifteen years ago, and now apply it in new ways to achieve things that years ago I would have never considered to be possible. So be prepared to see, think and dream as we take this journey into unlocking knowledge that will open your eyes to what is a much bigger world. Don't be afraid and most importantly do not dismiss this concept just because you have not heard of it in the past. Just read on with an open mind!

You may find the next few pages a bit hard going, especially if you are not technically orientated, however, just slowly chip away at it, and if you get stuck, just reread that section, but don't get too bogged down with the technical stuff, I am just trying to emphasise a point.

Put simply, the law of attraction is simply the ideal that we attract into our life that which we think about the most. This chapter will look at the connection between establishing the link between the thought process and how it determines everything from our mood, to attracting physical and tangible items into our life.

To begin let me first talk about **energy**. It is important to understand that thought is energy. Energy is measured in frequencies, and frequencies for the definition of understanding are expressed as hertz. If you compare this to electricity, in Australia our electricity is measured or expressed as 240 Volts, 50 Hz. In America it is 110 Volts, 60 Hz, and the hertz is the amount of times or changes in directions per second. If you think of an Oscilloscope (a device which makes the shape of a voltage wave visible on a screen) and the waving patterns it shows, for each change of direction is a Hz. Radio waves are the same. The FM frequency for example, operates at mega hertz, but in reality radio waves are like electricity, but at a much higher frequency. Both travel at the speed of light and both follow one of the most basic laws of the universe, and that is they flow from a high source to a low source. Wherever there is a potential or difference, the energy will flow.

I like to think of it this way: In air-conditioning and refrigeration for example, when a temperature difference exists, the higher source will flow to the lower source or temperature. That's how the most basic refrigeration effect works, for example the evaporator in your refrigerator contains cold gas at around -5°C (when the compressor operates), the air within the fridge is around +4°C, as such the air is warmer, and therefore at a higher potential. Naturally the heat is **attracted** and drawn into the colder refrigerant. As is the case for the warmer product such as a bottle of water that has just been filled and placed in the refrigerator, the water in the bottle is warmer then the surrounding air, so the heat actually flows from the product, into the air, into the refrigerant.

On a much larger scale, think about our sun, and the distance from earth. The sun is extremely hot, thousands of degrees in temperature, and we all know space is cold, ranging in temperature to the proximity of a source of radiant heat. For example at the extremes of our solar system or deep space, the temperature is a low as -273°C or 0°Kelvin. However, it is warmer in close proximity to earth and our sun, around -90°C. The point is the heat follows exactly the same law of the universe. Heat is energy: it will flow whenever a difference exists.

The above examples show the very point you need to understand in order to proceed. Energy flows from a high source to a low source. Now here is where you need to let go of old conditioning and thinking. Expand this concept to understand that everything is energy and nothing rests, everything has a frequency. Even a solid rock, if you were to look at it under an electron microscope you would see the atoms and neutrons buzzing around in a predetermined pattern, it is moving, it has energy and it would be measured in a very low frequency.

At the opposite end of the frequency spectrum is thought. It is now possible to measure thought and the associated brain activity as brain waves. So if you consider that solid objects represent the lowest end of the frequency spectrum, and thought waves represent the highest end of the spectrum, you can begin to categorise anything in-between. It is just like the three states of matter: solid, liquid and gaseous states.

So how can this understanding of physics and science improve our knowledge of oneself? Well it is simply by understanding that we are at one with nature, we are in harmony with our surroundings and environment. How naive to think that we as a race of people can pollute our atmosphere with the thousands of tonnes of CO_2 and green house gases on a daily basis, without causing damaging effects. You see we are living in a symbiotic relationship with this planet. Any increase in understanding is a good thing, but my point is that we are all linked. We are all made from the same carbon that has been on this planet for billions of years, and this now leads us to the next point, that energy and matter can never be destroyed.

Think about this, the carbon molecules and water (H_2O) that we are made from, have existed on this planet for billions of years. It is possible that some of the very molecules within us may well have manifested themselves as a dinosaur millions of years before. Now I am not suggesting we are in any way related. I am simply enforcing the idea that everything from the energy and matter that we are made of has always been here and always will be.

This analogy can also be used to understand the popular issue of "green house gases" and "global warming". It is not my intention to lecture on these environmental issues as there are those who are far better suited than I; however, I feel it is important to understand this point. It illustrates the very essence of this chapter which is to understand vibration and attraction and for that matter the first chapter on accountability. Surely we must take responsibility for our effects on this planet, after all it is the human race that is consuming fossil fuel at an increasing rate, and any time you burn fossil fuel you unlock and release CO_2 and other green house gases. Permit me to elaborate as this ties in everything that I have mentioned previously.

In my role as an industry leader, and together with my understanding of energy consumption within a building, (after all I am an accredited energy auditor); I have developed the following understanding. In this role I often find myself performing lectures discussing "The Building Code of Australia" (known as the BCA) and the recently implemented section on "energy efficiency" which is referred to as Section J of the BCA.

To help in providing a visual representation, I use a power point presentation that not only discusses and explains the various section of the BCA but I make reference to the excellent work of Al Gore, and the movie *An Inconvenient Truth*. In this movie Gore provides information in a graphical representation depicting the increase of CO_2 over the past 600,000 years. The graph shows a fairly constant fluctuation following a natural cycle, however, since the industrialisation of mankind, the increase is quite dramatic, and is continuing to increase. I focus on CO_2 because the increase is irrefutable, and the consequence to us human beings is disastrous. Currently, as I write these words, the CO_2 level in the ambient air is around 360ppm (parts per million). Now so this number means something to you, and the audience that I am delivering my presentation to, I give the example that in an enclosed room such as the lecture room I would be talking in, the CO_2 level is continuously increasing due to the occupancy of myself and the audience. This would, or at least should, be designed for in the air-conditioning equipment, in that a fixed percentage of **outdoor air** is introduced, or if it is a more sophisticated air-conditioning system it may employ a CO_2 sensing device and open a motorised damper, thus increasing the quantity of outdoor air into the occupied space.

However, no matter how it is provided, a minimum quantity of outdoor air is actually a legal requirement under the BCA, but the outdoor air is introduced in order to dilute the increasing levels of CO_2 in the occupied room. It follows that the BCA makes provision for different usage, i.e. more occupied areas have different classification, namely a lecture room or classroom are classified as a class 9b space, and would have occupancy of one person per two metres squared of occupied space. For each person, fifteen litres per second per person must be introduced in order to comply with the BCA.

An office for example has a lower occupancy, at one person per ten metres squared, and a lower quantity of ten litres per person is required. The very point that I am trying to demonstrate, is that outdoor air is introduced to reduce the build up of CO_2 due to the occupancy of the room; however, this only works because the incoming outdoor air has a lower quantity of CO_2 then the space to which it is being delivered to, namely 360ppm. Should this level increase, more outdoor air will have to be delivered to achieve the same result.

I use this example for good reason. No doubt you have all be in an enclosed room with a high occupancy and after a short period of time you feel stuffy, the sensation of falling asleep gets stronger and stronger. Well this is simply the CO_2 levels increasing. If you are exposed to a CO_2 level above 1000ppm we lose the conscious ability to focus and concentrate, and ultimately will fall asleep. And if we are in a high CO_2 environment for prolonged periods, permanent brain damage and even death can occur when levels exceed 5000ppm. Now keep in mind here, if we breathe in air that contains CO_2 at levels of 360ppm, it has increased to around 4000ppm by the time we breathe it out. So basically, if this is the effect that one person has on the air we breathe, imagine the effect several people have in a small and non-ventilated space?

For this reason, a class 9b space is generally controlled to a level of 600ppm of CO_2 by the introduction of outdoor air through the air-conditioning system. My point here is: what happens if in forty years as predicted the outdoor air level of CO_2 is already at 600ppm?

So what is causing this dramatic increase of CO_2? Well it all goes back to the dinosaurs. Yes the Jurassic period.

Seventy million years ago, our planet earth was a very different place. Dinosaurs ruled the planet, humankind had not yet evolved. Scientists now believe that the CO_2 level at this time was around 1300 – 1400 parts per million, this is four times that of today's levels, and undoubtedly we could not have survived for long if we were there.

> **"Every time you breathe in, thank a tree."**
>
> *John Wright*

During this time the earth was much warmer, the "green house" effect was resulting in heat being trapped by a blanket of smoke and ash from a period of volcano activity which is believed to be the predominant reason for the elevated levels of CO_2. As the planet was quite warm there were no polar ice caps and this resulted in low or no ocean currents. The ocean temperatures were also much warmer and the oceans were green due to the prolific build up of algal growth; just imagine how different it was from the world we live in today.

However the algal growth provided a very important task, in that the green cells within the algae would use the sunlight and through photosynthesis flourish, the algae being a plant life form would then feed on the CO_2 and expel oxygen. (Again you see the symbiotic relationship we share with plant life.) Eventually, as the algae would die, it would settle and the sediment level would increase due to the prolonged settlement of the dying algae, layer upon layer upon layer. Evidence of this very process has been witnessed in the gulf of New Mexico even today. However, with continuous depositing the sediment levels became so dense that the weight of compression over millions of years resulted in the production of crude oil, coal and shale, and with additional and extraordinary compression, the result was natural gas. So over the course of several millions of years the level of CO_2

reduced to pre-industrialisation age levels.

The problem is this: whenever fossil fuel is burnt, and we seem to excel in that, the CO_2 that is locked up in the oil and gas is released into the atmosphere. The rate of release is not sustainable and is a direct result of humankind. This process is beautifully depicted in a documentary called *A Crude Awakening: The Oil Crash*, the story behind the production of crude oil.

Again, I must stress, it is not my intention to sound like an extreme environmentalist, but I think we all must take on board that it is our responsibility to be aware of the impact we have on our planet. We must develop a sustainable lifestyle. At this rate we are only creating a problem for our children to resolve and, for that matter, suffer from the effects of our neglect and ignorance.

It is truly my wish that by overcoming ignorance with awareness, and by highlighting the point that each and every one of us, is in some way responsible for this situation. Consider the above effect on a "global" or "macro" scale. There is a parallel to our own mind, albeit on a "micro" scale. Apart from the obvious link of accountability, we live in a symbiotic relationship with the planet, and our current lifestyle is causing a long term problem. This is "cause and effect" in action. You see we can choose to do nothing about it (with disastrous effects) or we can choose to band together and solve the problem, and learn from our mistakes and live a more sustainable lifestyle. But it is our choice!

Think about some of the mistakes that you have made in the past, and what effect they may have had on your situation today. I know that I have made many, but as long as we learn from our mistakes, or let that outcome increase our awareness and choose not to do that again, we are learning. To me this is the very definition of learning – learning of life lessons. Think about the previous chapter and the analogy of looking at life as if you were looking in a rear-vision mirror while driving your car. Make the choice to learn from your mistakes and alter our thinking with increased awareness and you will alter the outcome and as such learn from that mistake. In this analogy, you have changed your course with anticipation of an approaching obstacle and that is how you are supposed to drive your car, isn't it?

Back to "vibration and attraction", in the previous analogies and background stories I deliberately highlighted these two key words. Remember, everything vibrates, nothing rests. So the law of **vibration** and **attraction** is attracting energy or things that you are in "harmony with" into your life. How is it that a massive oak tree can grow from a tiny acorn seed? It is vibration and attraction. The seed falls from the tree and is fortunate to land in an environment that is conducive to its development. It will attract the things it needs to grow, namely, nutrition from the surrounding soil, moisture and the like. Eventually the seed will develop roots to further absorb these key elements. Before long it will shoot out of the ground with green foliage that as we know uses photosynthesis to produce the energy it needs to grow.

If the same acorn seed were to fall on a solid pavement or on a large rock and was not able to attract the elements that it needs to grow, it will very quickly decay and die. The same can be said for our life and for that matter our mind! We are growing, learning and developing, or we are decaying, rotting and generally going backwards.

At the beginning of this chapter I mentioned how energy flows from a high source to a low source. The acorn seed when it is surrounded by all of the things it needs to grow, will allow the potential energy in the surrounding environment to flow to it, and allow it to grow on its predetermined path. But the key here is this attraction: it will only attract things that are in harmony with it. Think of it this way, when you tune your radio to your favourite station, you actually adjust the frequency, so that only the frequency you want to listen to is drawn from the air, into the antenna and into the radio. Imagine the mess of noise if all frequencies and radio stations were played at once, it would be just a mess of scrambled noise. But you see that's how it works, we can choose to listen to exactly the radio station we want or tune the TV to only the station we want, through **selective attraction**.

So now for the **BIG Question**: how can we use what you have just learnt to improve your life and achieve the results that you desire?

Well the answer is contained in the above key words. **The results that you desire:** at this point let go of old conditioning and thinking and focus on this new concept. We have established the fact that your results are the product of your decisions and thinking up to this point, But consider this: with an increased awareness and understanding it will become obvious that you can choose to have whatever outcome you want. That's right, if you choose to have a greater success and an increased abundance in your life, all you need to do is to **think** about it and the law of vibration and attraction will deliver it to you! Still struggling with this concept? Well let me elaborate.

When we think we think in pictures, but as I have mentioned above, thinking is the conversion of a single picture or thought to an electrical energy or measurable vibration. Imagine it this way: we have all heard of or seen with our own eyes the result of two people whose thought pattern or level of vibration are in harmony. A good example of this is identical twins, and how they are often able to share each others feelings, visions and thoughts. This is a concept that I have no trouble in understanding, as on several occasions I have witnessed this amazing process for myself. Perhaps the most recent example of this very point took place a few months ago.

Ben, who is a colleague of mine in our consulting firm, was handing over a project to me as he was just about to get married and I was overseeing the project while he was on holiday. The project involved the replacement of two chillers at a large TAFE project. Ben and I were discussing the existing chillers, when I asked him, what was the make of the old chillers? Without Ben saying a word, I received a flash of an image, the image was of a beige chillier (suggesting to me that the make was of LUKE manufacture). However, and more importantly, I asked Ben what was with the gray coloured compressor on the left? This particular chiller had one of the two compressors rebuilt some years prior, and it was painted gray. Now the interesting thing is that I had not been into this plant room, or even to this particular campus before, I had no prior knowledge of the compressor being rebuilt. But I could clearly see this image. Fortunately for me, I shared this experience with several people in my office, one of which was my current apprentice/student David or as I like to call him, my Padawin learner. Some weeks later, David and I were actually in this plant room and there it was, this beige Luke chiller with its gray compressor on the left hand side.

Now this is not the only example of this occurrence in my life, however it is probably the best example for me as it involved several of my colleagues and we still get a chuckle about it today. But you see that is how it works. How is it possible that two people can share the same image or thought? Well I don't know exactly how it works as I am not an expert on the human brain, but I do know this: if you just except that it **does** happen and do not reject that it can happen and embrace this ideal and concept, I believe you actually allow more of the same to occur. You see this is something that I have complete **faith** in, and faith is simply: **the belief in the impossible and the ability to see the invisible, to achieve the incredible**.

You may or may not be able to repeat a similar story. In fact, I have observed a direct link between how successful someone is (and I am not measuring success in just financial terms) and an understanding of just about everything that I have written about up to this point. Most people that I have talked to about this topic can recall a similar story, and as I have mentioned earlier, that's the definition of learning, not repeating word for word, but actually involving a feeling from listening.

The key phrase here is "involving a **feeling**". You see, thinking about something alone does not make it happen. However the more you think about something the more energy you give to that thought. The more frequently you focus on one thought the more potent it becomes. Eventually with sustained thought you attach feeling to this thought and this is how you make that thought so powerful, its energy at a particular frequency is released into the universe. So the point here is simply this, the more potent the thought, the more energy you associate to that thought, the stronger the energy behind that thought, the higher the probability that someone else has in receiving that thought. And that is how it works, a subliminal psychic connection, the very essence of the **law of attraction**. We will discuss this point more in the following "Goal Setting" chapter, but simply think of it this way. Praying is simply a form of goal setting: you think about something that you want to achieve or obtain, you do it so often and with so much energy behind it that you will generally obtain your desires. That's how it works.

I truly believe that we get out of life what we want. The trouble is, we allow our thoughts to wander resulting in confused and irrelevant thoughts, or put simply, enough energy, just misdirected. A beautiful analogy for this is think of a small battery-powered light globe that is only, say eight watts. Now on its own and in an open environment the resulting light that is emitted from the globe is quit dull, all of the light energy is able to spread evenly in all directions. Now picture the same globe in a torch, the light energy is channelled and directed in a focused beam, with a much brighter outcome. So you see most of us have enough energy, we just misdirect it. Every time you focus, you actually channel and focus the thought, making it more powerful.

Here is an example of the power of a thought, once you involve feelings, to attract a physical object into your life. I use a physical object, but the same process can be used to achieve pretty much anything you can think of.

Let's say you have the desire to have a new car. Now this is something that we all have thought about at some time in our life. Let's look at what is actually happening. First of all you see a brand new car on the road, or see a commercial on the TV, and you go wow, *that car looks great, I have to get me one of those. I can really see myself driving that car or wouldn't I look great behind the wheel?*

At this point we have two choices, we can either keep

wishing and hoping that one day we will be lucky enough to afford a car, just like that one. But you see this thought process simply transfers the desire to a future time, with no certainty and just wishful thinking. It is pretty much guaranteed that you will not obtain the new car. But imagine the difference if you allow yourself to actually test drive the car? What you're doing is involving the physical emotions and senses, by driving the car you smell the unique smell of a new car, you feel the joy of actually driving the car, and when you drive past a shop window, you actually see your self driving the new car. All of these things are involving our senses and with all senses involved our feelings unite to focus the desire and thought, and the potency of that thought has been shifted ten fold. But it does not end there. You're so impressed with the car and now you want it even more then you did before you went on the test drive, so you take a brochure home with you. Every time you look at that brochure the memory of the driving experience comes flooding back, the emotion of wanting the car is strengthened. But what you are actually doing is giving more potency to the original thought, and when you do this over and over again, it becomes a habit.

So just with this simple analogy, you can see the difference between the two thought processes. It is literally a choice, how much do you really want that thing (can be anything) in you life? Look around at the things that you have attracted into your life, can you attach a similar story to these things?

So time now to look at the final step of the law of attraction, and that is **actions**. The above analogy demonstrates the link between thoughts and feelings, but consider this: thoughts and feelings alone are not enough to achieve what it is that we want. Allow me to elaborate.

Continuing on with the new car analogy, you have been for the test drive, you have the glossy brochures, your desire for the car is at a peak. However, you are not sure if you can afford it, or are not sure if your current income will cover the repayments if you lease the car. This is where the final and most important element comes into play, and I have deliberately left it until now to talk about as it will involve all of the understanding from this entire chapter to fully establish the importance of the subconscious mind.

Believe it or not, you will actually **attract** the solution. We have established in this analogy that the desire for the new car is present, but lack the final part, the purchase or uncertainty associated with the financial transaction. But this is where the sub-conscious mind is so powerful. You already know what it is you need to do to earn the extra income, or attract the additional funds. What is of interest here is the sub-conscious mind tells you what you need to do, it is the little voice in your head that pops up from time to time and advises us, don't do this and so on. But the important thing to understand is simply that it invokes the sub-conscious mind, you do not have to worry about working harder or focusing on making more money, by simply having faith and believing it will come, it will because you attract it.

We have established the link between thoughts and feelings resulting in actions, but just as sure as it works in a positive result or outcome, it also works in reverse, that is to say, if you focus on a negative outcome, like worrying about debt or lack of money that is exactly what you will attract. This is why you must be careful with what you wish for: if you focus on debt and more hard times, that's what you attract, and this is why most people seem to get caught up in a never-ending circle of debt, bills and worries.

> **"We either make ourselves happy or miserable. The amount of work is the same."**
>
> *Carlos Castaneda*

Don't just believe me, actually think to your self and ask yourself, what is your normal state of thoughts?

Are you typically thinking about what you don't want? Guess what, you're only going to get more of the same. If on the other hand you have already mastered this concept, you will be aware of this fact, and your state of thought will be positive and will generally achieve the results and outcomes that you desire.

It is our **actions** that truly define us, and as I have demonstrated, our actions are simply a result of our **thoughts**, this manifests as our **feelings** and thus determines our actions and that is how it works, it always has, and always will. Perhaps one of the most powerful quotes that I have come across in my studies in this field is:

> **"All that we are is a result of what we have thought."**
>
> Buddha (563 BC–483 BC)

The law of attraction not only works with things and objects, but I am firmly of the opinion that it is most powerful with people rather than physical objects. We have discussed how the mind and thought is **energy** and how we can be in "harmony with" somebody else and their vibration. Let me tell you the story about how I actually attracted partners into my life.

After my divorce, I felt (as most men in the same situation) somewhat lacking in self-confidence and apprehensive around women, after all it is normal to carry some emotional scarring after such a life changing event. For me, this was a time when my subconscious mind automatically drew from the teachings that I had been exposed to, and now that I look back at that time, I guess there was a reason why I met the women that I did. Now don't get me wrong here, this is not meant to be a "tell all" about my sex life, however it serves as an example of how by using the laws of attraction you can in a very short period of time completely change your emotional state. Remember, my definition of emotional state is the thoughts, feelings and actions that are the manifestation of your predominate thoughts.

I guess I had been separated from my wife for about six months. It was April 2005, the time of the Clipsal 500, a V8 super car four day motor car racing event held in the streets of Adelaide. I had been fortunate enough to be the guest of an air-conditioning supplier and after enjoying a very full day of "beer-and bloke-ship" the group I was with went out to a nearby restaurant for dinner. Now keep in mind this was my first outing as a single guy, up until then I had deliberately retreated to my "emotional cave" and had chosen not to venture out for fear of judgement and rejection, after all it was my emotional state that was lacking at this time.

Jenni's story:

I will never forget the circumstances of this particular evening, when this attractive and petite lady came over to our table and started talking to some of the guys in our group. I can even recall saying to one of the guys "wow just imagine being with her, I wish I had the courage to talk to her". I watched a good friend of mine who was in our group, who kept looking over to me, and referring to me in his conversation. I later found out he was actually explaining how I would make a good catch, as I was single and a good bloke (his words not mine). Before long she had started to talk to me and introduced herself as Jenni and I responded "Jenni with an 'I' right?"

You see Jenni was actually doing some marketing as she owned a company that embroidered company logos and the like, and I thought she was simply trying to drum up some more business. Anyway after some small talk, Jenni left to go back to her own table. After a few hours, we had all finished our meals and as a group we were looking to continue the evening's festivities in the form of a "pub crawl". As we were leaving, Jenni came racing up to the table, looked me straight in the eyes, passed me her business card with her left hand and shock my hand with her right hand, and I will never forget she said, "here is my card, I really want you to call me". Wow, and in front of all my colleagues, needless to say, this helped to improve my emotional state and self-confidence.

Naturally I called Jenni the next working day and within a few days had dated and before too long we were in a relationship. I guess now that I look back at this time, Jenni was in fact in a similar state of mind as she had also recently broken up from her husband. The relationship that we enjoyed helped both of us to realise that we could be appreciated by someone else, our self worth improved, and from my perspective I enjoyed getting involved with somebody new and being involved in their life, experiencing their joys, problems and hard-ships. In that period, I learnt so much about human nature and strengthened my own beliefs about the human mind and habitual thinking.

Jenni and I were together for about a year. For various reasons we broke up, but we still saw each other casually for a further six months. But in my mind the relationship was not going in a direction that would enable a long term commitment. I have no regrets about the time we spent together: it was a period of learning, loving and new-found intimacy which enabled us to grow emotionally from the experience.

The next period of my life was one of emotional self-exile, I deliberately did not want to go out to meet just anybody. I immersed myself in my work and on the weekends, I would dedicate myself to my kids. I needed some time to sort out in my mind exactly what I was looking for. During this time I met a few girls through a colleague at work, but nothing eventuated. I guess because I did not know what I was looking for and I also realised that I had not actually spent much time on my own since my divorce. After all you can not be comfortable in a relationship until you are comfortable with yourself. The best way to see if you are is to spend time on your own, this way you very quickly find out what makes you happy!

It was about this time when I was introduced to *The Secret*. At first I came across a copy of the DVD, and watched it over and over again. Then I bought a copy of the book, and began to read it over and over again. By applying the law of attraction to my business life, my industry reputation certainly flourished. It was at this time when I had performed several speaking engagements with my industry standing dramatically improved. However as my career was now at a point where I wanted it, I wanted to see if I could use the law of attraction to actually attract a new partner!

I will never forget using this time to focus on what kind of partner I was actually looking for, I can clearly remember doing the visualisation techniques (I will discuss visualisation in much greater depth in the next chapter). I needed to clearly define the type of person, with all of the attributes that in my mind would make for an interesting and successful relationship. Then by using the law of attraction, I had faith that this person would be attracted into my life. Now I guess if you're reading this for the first time, your thoughts would be something like "what an extremist or idealist" but let me assure you this stuff works. Only when in my mind I was ready to meet someone, I did!

> **"When the student is ready,
> the teacher appears."**
>
> *Anonymous*

I can recall lying in bed one night after reading a few pages of *The Secret*, when I was "putting it out there into the universe" when the image of some one popped into my head. You see I had actually met this person some weeks prior during a business meeting, but when Annie's image appeared in my mind, I knew I needed to act on it.

Annie's Story:

Annie was a project manager for an organisation that we had been working with. We had, over several weeks, gotten to know each other reasonably well. I knew that she was quite intelligent, but also seemed to have the great gift in reading people, which was an attribute considering her career. She was incredibly attractive, I can recall being impressed with her dress sense and she always appeared impeccably presented. No wonder when I was visualising all of the attributes that I was looking for, her image popped into my mind.

As this one particular project we were working on was nearing completion, I found myself and Annie in this new laboratory, discussing data points and hub servers (work stuff) when I knew this was the right time to act on my thoughts. This gave me the courage to ask Annie out for a coffee, after all what could be the worst thing to happen? For her to say "no" of course. Fortunately she said yes, and during our discussion over coffee I found myself talking about some of the concepts discussed in this book. She sat there and listened to what I had to say, and actually agreed with me and seemed to keep up with all of the ideas we discussed. Her positive outlook on life and grasp on the "laws of the universe" (as I call them) blew me away and only served to increase my attraction to her. After about forty-five minutes we needed to get back to work, so I put all of my cards on the table and asked Annie if she wanted to go out to dinner.

She said "yes" and a few days later we enjoyed a wonderful meal and stimulating conversation. I had met my match, someone I could talk to, and someone who gave me as much by talking about their understanding of people and the human mind. How enjoyable and refreshing it was to meet someone with this powerful mind-set, this was exactly what I was looking for at that time.

So you see, it does work, if you set your mind to it you can achieve anything you want! Relationships are a fluid thing, always in motion, always changing, evolving, with each having their own desires (which is a good thing). The key is to communicate and focus on being happy. Stimulate each other's wants, needs and desires and keep it fresh and exciting. This is where I have learnt that we get it wrong, why the divorce rate is so high. We seem to get bored and tired with our partners and so complacency creeps in. Understand that relationships are as I call it "fluid", "in motion", not cast in stone. Review your relationships, don't just accept that you have been together since your were married or for seemingly countless years. A successful relationship is just like a successful business, you need to work on it every day.

In this chapter we have discussed a great many things, now you can see the difficulty I was facing, how can I communicate the idea of the "law of vibration and attraction"? Hopefully by telling the stories I have about my life, you now understand the relationship between thinking and results. By recalling the first chapter on accountability and applying the lessons in the second chapter about living life based on the past, you can now clearly see that we do not need to live our life based on past events. As Winston Churchill once said, "**You create your own universe as you go along**". Just think about that for a while!

Here is a beautiful passage that I have come across and want to share with you. I came across this passage during one of the Bob Proctor seminars I attended many years ago, it captures the essence of this chapter and indeed the entire book:

Let us not look back in anger, nor look forward in fear, but look around us with awareness.

Wow! What a powerful, meaningful and profound passage. Try and remember this passage, and use it to help you through the tough times ahead.

As I re-read these words, I am reminded of the very

reason that I decided to write this book. You see it is now some months since I wrote the above chapter and I find myself actually taking comfort in my own words. As I mention above, life and relationships are a fluid concept. Remember how in the previous page I was talking about Annie, and how important to me she is, well as a further example of how life can and does take uncontrolled turns, we are no longer together.

You see, you can maintain and control your own thoughts, feelings and actions, but a relationship involves two people. It is impossible to control your partner's state of mind, and quite often the same outcome or long term desire is not shared.

As you can imagine, when Annie and I broke up, I was shattered. I guess I have always been the type of guy who wears their heart on their sleeve. I am outward with my emotions and feelings, a friend of mine mocks me because of this, however, it is who I am! Some months have passed since writing the previous words, and I suspect many months, possible years will pass before I complete this project. But by writing my thoughts and interjecting from time to time, it only serves to strengthen the very essence of the point that I am trying to make. As far as relationships go, I am certain I will meet another partner, for it is firmly my belief that it is better to have loved and lost, then to not have loved at all! And I am not afraid to risk falling in love again, because it is as simple as this: **to risk nothing is to have nothing**. Sometimes you have to put yourself out there, and relish that fear that comes from pushing the boundaries, but much more on that topic in a later chapter entitled I.Q. vs E.Q.

Life is precious, make the most of every day, and realise that not all circumstances and events can be controlled, bad things do happen. What we are talking about here is the ability to pick yourself up, dust yourself off, and move forward in the direction that is required to achieve your goals and desires. **For it is what we do in the face of adversity or when things go wrong (and they will) that defines who we are!**

Be true to yourself and your goals and the law of vibration and attraction will ensure that you get what you want! It always has and always will, that's why it is a *"law of the universe"*.

4 VISUALISATION TO DEVELOP GOAL SETTING

We have touched on visualisation and goal setting in the previous chapter, but let's have a closer look.

The word "visualise" means "to see in one's mind" therefore by definition and by understanding just how powerful the human mind is, it make sense that we can pretty much visualise anything that we want.

I have tremendous respect for authors of novels who have the ability to conceive in their mind complete and epic stories, take George Lucas for example, with the *Star Wars* series of movies. As a child I grew up with this phenomenon, in some ways it was the reason I started to research for myself the meaning of the "force" and the philosophies behind the force and its relationship to today's laws and beliefs. My research led me to discover that the Jedi knight draws similarities to the ancient Japanese "Samurai Warrior". In fact the word samurai actually means "to serve" or "servant of the people". However my point is this: how amazing that George Lucas could take an experience based on the history of our planet and make it involve a galaxy far far away! A classic good versus evil story, but fundamentally a story conceived in one man's mind! He had devotion and persistence to convert the image he had visualised into the six epic movies that portray the full story.

One can only imagine the difficulties he faced over the many years (almost thirty years between the original *Star Wars* movie and *Episode III – Revenge of the Sith* the final movie made). This example serves to highlight one man's passion and unshakeable faith and desire to portray a story as **he visualised**, which is the essence of this chapter.

Try and recount a similar story about something that is familiar and close to you! Remember, the essence of learning something new is easier when you can relate the topic to yourself and your own life and interests. As I mentioned earlier in this book, it is not the ability to recall the words you hear or read word for word that defines learning, it is actually what those words mean to you, your own example of your life experience that you think about that brings further clarity and lean to the subject you are exposed to.

Visualisation is an activity that occurs in your mind, the more you practise it, the better you become at it. It starts with simply thinking about a single thought and then allowing the thought to play out like a movie in your mind from start to conclusion.

Through visualisation you can imagine the consequence of any circumstance that has not yet occurred, it is an unwritten story that you are the author of. Nobody else can see it, only you create it and allow it to evolve into the outcome that you direct it to.

Some would consider this "day dreaming" but I like to think of it as allowing the creative process the forum to grow and develop. You see, the possibilities and directions you can go with this concept are limitless. Some more skilful at this are able to combine the art of meditation with visualisation to focus on the subject in a very relaxed state. By meditating you relax the subconscious mind, and this is the part of the mind where visualisation occurs, and by doing so allow a more graphic and visual process to occur, which in turn increases the potency of the original thought.

Remember the example in the previous chapter about the purchase of a new car? Just imagine how potent that process would be if you involve all of the physical and tangible feelings along with the ability to visualise yourself in possession and driving the new car? What you are actually doing is building new synaptic connections in your brain. You see the human brain finds it difficult to distinguish between visualising an activity and actually doing the activity. The more times you visualise or see yourself perform this activity, or in this case see yourself driving the new car, the stronger the synaptic pathways become.

In the BBC documentary *The Human Mind*, this concept is beautifully explained and related to a young English gymnast, who by successfully using the visualisation techniques as shown to her by her coach, performs a very difficult routine on the parallel bars. The more often she visualises the routine, the stronger the synaptic connections become in her brain (synaptic connection being a pathway built from neurological cells, to serve as a conductive path way for the electrical activity that is our thought process). Her brain believes that she has now performed this new routine several times, and the various and complex manoeuvres involving all of her muscles firing at just the right time has already been established, and when it actually comes time perform the exercise for the first time, she is able to perform it successfully as if she had practiced it several times earlier.

So just imagine applying this technique to something that you may not have been able to successfully achieve in the past. It does not matter if it is a new goal, a new skill or even a new state of mind. It works in the exact same way as outlined in the two above examples.

OK so let us now apply this new found knowledge to the topic at hand – **goal setting**.

Firstly, you must have a goal in mind, let's say you want to double your salary and you are in a commission-only sales situation. I chose this example for the simplistic nature of the financial outcome, however the theory works equally well with any goal. Now like the analogy of the light globe in the torch, you must only focus on this one goal, don't allow yourself to be distracted by countless other thoughts and influences. Most importantly do not allow yourself to be distracted by negative thoughts from someone else saying this can not be achieved. Have faith that you will achieve what you set out to achieve, put into practice all of the points that we have discussed up to this point.

Now clear your mind of all superfluous and irrelevant thoughts, focus and concentrate on visualising the thought of seeing yourself earning the additional income. See the increased lifestyle it brings with it, see yourself enjoying all of the spoils that you want (hence the reason for the additional income).

The more often you do this exercise the stronger you make the synaptic connection, which is the brain believing this is the new state, albeit that it is only visualisation at this point. But remember the brain can not distinguish between reality and a habit or memory developed by visualisation alone. So naturally the more graphic and "visual" you make your image, the more real it will appear in your mind.

In this example we are developing the goal of doubling your income, by seeing yourself actually receiving your pay cheque with the additional amount, then seeing yourself with the things around you that the additional income will provide. You very quickly set up the state of "expiation" where you expect to earn more money and have a higher degree of comfort in your life. If you continue to do this for long enough, and in my opinion it takes twenty eight days to develop a habit, eventually a difference appears between the visualised outcome and the reality or previous situation. Our subconscious mind starts to kick in and compares the old ways with the new conditioning, this is why it is so important to give as much clarity and definition to your thoughts when developing the visual image that you have been working with.

By attaching emotion to the new lifestyle, you actually choose the new conditioning as the desired state; as such you have successfully altered your state of consciousness. Relating this to the previous chapter about energy and vibration, you have raised your vibratory state to a point where the new conditioning takes precedence over the older state, and as we now know a higher energy level will always flow towards the lower state, that is a "law of the universe", eventually replacing the old state with new expiations and desires. The rest simply falls into place, with new expiations in place. The subconscious mind will act to make you perform what it is that you do to earn your income. You see it does not matter what you do, your subconscious mind will help you to perform your chosen career in such a way that your expectant results will be different, you will instantly and automatically change the way you work, this will deliver the change of income and deliver the desired outcome.

Don't make the mistake of assuming that by simply asking for an increased pay cheque that you will receive one, this is all about the subconscious mind automatically altering your activities to enable you to earn more money.

In the previous chapter we talked about thoughts, feelings and actions. In this example the **thoughts** component is in the form of visualisation. By using physical reminders such as a "goal card" we improve on the **feelings** component. So what is a "goal card"? Quite simply a goal card is a small card on which your immediate goal is written, in your hand writing. The idea is that you read the card, therefore refreshing the goal in your mind every time you read the card. With the intent being continuous referral to the card, as often as possible, namely twenty to thirty times a day, the idea or goal is imprinted into the mind, therefore helping with the **thought** component of the process.

Remember in the previous chapter, when looking at the purchase of a new car, by test driving the car we involve all of the senses, the smell, the feeling of satisfaction when driving the car, all of theses feelings can be channelled to help with the new goal of doubling your income. The idea is to give as much clarity to your goal as possible. So through visualisation you can now clearly see yourself earning the new amount, you can see the better lifestyle that will come with the additional income. So now let's look at the final component, your **actions**.

I have previously mentioned that your actions are a result of your predominant thoughts. By now you should be able to see the link here between all three components: thoughts, feelings and actions. You see your actions in the past were as a result of the past thoughts, with the new conditioning and new thoughts, new actions will naturally follow. This is quite simply how it works, your actions will change. Remember the passage I quoted from Buddha?

"All that we are is the result of what we have thought."

That's not just a cute saying, it's the truth!

You can truly change the very essence of "**YOU**" with this understanding. While this particular example relates to improved income, I have observed people change their personality by this very concept. With a full and deep understanding of these very ideals, you can be, do and have anything you want. You just need the faith and commitment to "make it so".

I have one final point to finish off this scenario about additional income and money. I have observed that people tend to think that simply improving or increasing their income will solve all of their money troubles. Nothing could be further from the truth! In reality we pretty much spend as much money as we make, so by simply earning more money, the natural state would be to spend any additional funds. By all means use this knowledge on goal setting to help you achieve a greater income, but believe me, a greater income alone will not improve your quality of life if you are debt bound, or have not developed a savings plan or repayment schedule to get out of debt.

If you, like me, are looking to improve your quality of life, then you will understand that money should **not** be your central focus. A truly "**Rich Life**" is not measured by the amount of money or positions you have accumulated along the way. A "rich life" is measured by happiness and joyful living along the way. Now "joyful living" is something that is truly unique to each of us and will be different for everyone, but please do not get confused or deliriously think that more money will make you happy!

A holistic approach to finances is required. Yes a higher income can help you to reach your financial goals faster, but you must have a financial goal. For most of us we work until retirement age (around fifty-five to sixty years of age) and hopefully by then the debts are paid, namely the mortgage on the house and cars and the like, and you have sufficient funds invested, so as the income derived by this investment provides enough "cash flow" to allow you the lifestyle you choose. The key point here is the understanding that we should be looking for "financial freedom" for when this is successfully achieved true financial freedom is found.

Simply earning more money when you are in debt, will not set you free, for it is human nature to simply increase your spending in a proportional fashion. You must develop a savings plan in that you pay yourself first. Sounds simple, but yes you actually pay yourself, say 10 percent (or more) of your income into a savings account, or similar investment account. It will not take long before you have some serious coin behind you, and believe me the confidence and credibility that comes with money behind you is amazing, your self-worth is improved and the image of yourself changes from somebody who is always spending more than they make to a positive self-image of yourself, working towards a financial goal.

At this point I must stress that you should seek out the help of a professional financial planner to help you establish your own goals and savings plans, as every one has a unique circumstance and desired outcome. At this point it is simply my intention to establish the link between financial freedom and financial independence in an effort to increase ones self-worth and increase your self-image. A certified financial planner will be able to show you the most effective way (tailored to your circumstances) to obtain your own financial freedom.

One final point I want to mention while we are talking about money and financial freedom, did you know that there are only two ways of making money? Most people mistakenly believe there are hundreds, but in reality there are only two:

    1. Money working for you.
    2. People working for you.

It sounds almost too simple to be true, but it is. The first point, money working for you, can be as simple as your own house increasing in equity, or playing the stock market to improve your share portfolio.

There are several ways to achieve the same thing, increasing equity in something at a greater rate than inflation and growing at a higher rate than the input cost, namely interest, fees, charges and the like.

The second point is equally as straight forward. As individuals we are limited to our own results, you may be the most motivated person on the planet, but you are still limited by your own self. When you have people working for you, then you're efforts can be multiplied by the number of people employed. Take a multi-national corporation for example and compare the turnover and resulting profitability to a small family company or one person show. I have observed this very point in our own business. Not only are Brad, Tony and I the major share holders, but our succession plan involves most of our employees, in that the majority are themselves shareholders, in turn giving them ownership in the company. And I will add that our own bank uses our company as a shining example of succession planning when teaching this concept to their clients.

Now seeing there are only two ways of making money, it makes sense to have both of them working for you. As outlined above, I am happy with the second point of people working for you, but the following is an account of how I would make the first point of money working for you come into play.

Throughout this book, I have accounted stories from my own life and the people around me in an effort to highlight a particular point. I now want to tell you the story about how I set myself a goal (and it was a big one) and how I used all of the points that we have looked at so far in this book to achieve that goal.

I have discussed previously in this book about my marriage break-up and how it effected me deeply, my finances were greatly affected also. I was fortunate in that I had a good income, and with what little money I was left with after the marriage break-up, I invested into my business. This is a point that I am truly grateful for as my return on this investment has proven to be a wise investment indeed, and with the guidance and advice from by business partner Brad (more about his influence in the following chapter) my financial goals were slowly being established and achieved. For example, at the time of writing these words, my combined worth resulting from the equity in my assets, equity in our business and superannuation, has now exceeded the equity as a couple when I was married. Now this is not too shabby considering it has only been three and a half years since my divorce!

However, I still was not completely happy with my personal life, in particular where I was living. You see since my marriage break-up, I had been renting a town house in Stirling in the Adelaide Hills. Don't get me wrong, it was a lovely place, in a beautiful suburb, but I felt that the real estate boom was passing me by, and without my own place to call my own I felt somewhat incomplete.

I will never forget the circumstances behind the decision to buy my own home. It was around August 2007 and I had been reading, or re-reading as the case may be, Bob Proctor's book *You Were Born Rich* and this one point about goal setting seemed to reach out to me. The chapter was actually called, the *Pat and Author story*, and as the name suggests, it was about two friends of Bob who did not have their own house and did not know how to go about achieving it. Bob preceded to help them with a check list of items that they must work on, namely, how much could they afford to borrow, how much deposit did they have, which in turn would direct them to the price bracket of house that they should be looking at. They truly did not believe they could own their own house, and this was causing them much sadness. After several discussions with Bob, they came to realise that they could in fact own their own house, they just needed to visualise what kind of house they wanted and make it their goal. They eventually set the goal to obtain and be living in their own house by Christmas. Wow, here I was in the similar time of year so I decided to make my new goal to find, purchase and be living in my own house by Christmas 2007.

Once the goal was established, I became passionate about it, and so it became my predominate thought, I could not only see myself in a new house, but believed I could achieve it in a short time frame. And this is why I mention this particular event, you see, all of the points I have talked about were now coming into play. I could visualise myself living in my own house, it became my predominant thought. I believed with every fibre of my being that it was possible. And as I write this particular paragraph, I am in my new home on Christmas holidays, well I actually moved in about two months ago, but I have not written much since moving in as that was my predominate thought at that time, so the writing of this book took second place.

In reality there were several obstacles, such as finding something that was affordable and provided for my needs, namely bachelor during the week, but with three kids on the weekends it needed to be big enough to accommodate the four of us, as well as a spare room for my gym. But undoubtedly the biggest obstacle was the banks. However, I sought the help of a broker whose job it was to deal with the banks, and before long all obstacles and heralds were one-by-one eliminated and my goal was achieved.

In writing these words I am reminded about a saying I picked up in one of the Bob Proctor seminars, from the French conqueror Napoleon:

> **I see only the objective;
> the obstacles must give way.**

But as Bob was quick to point out, use the saying but don't be like him, he was not a nice person.

Hopefully, you can relate to my story, as no doubt you have been able to achieve a goal in obtaining something that you were passionate about. Remember it is simply the ability to focus on the goal at the onset of the thought, using the techniques we have discussed to achieve the result, maintain persistence, but most importantly have faith that you will achieve your goal.

This approach can be used for anything! Try it for yourself, establish your own goal, re-read this chapter over and over again and go out with a new goal for yourself and achieve it! But above all do not under estimate the importance of having and establishing goals, for without goals we have nothing to aim for and in all likelihood only end up with more of the same, so how can we go about changing or improving our lives without a definitive path or direction?

Goals allow us to strive for self improvement, and by establishing short, medium and long term goals gives us what is called "check points on route" this is why it is better to start this creative process with a series of smaller goals until you have habitualised the effective use of goal setting.

Finally, understand the importance of establishing a time frame associated with each goal for it is my opinion that:

> **"Goal setting with out a firm time frame is just wishful thinking."**
>
> Kevin O'Reilly

5 EMPATHY

The word empathy, in my mind, relates more towards feelings and emotions rather than a simple "black and white" description, as such it may prove quite difficult to appropriately quantify for the definition of this chapter. However, I'll use a series of personal experiences to portray my understanding of this term, in order to properly discuss this most important element in the communication process.

In my opinion, empathy is not normally considered or associated with communication, in conversation, written or verbal. By this I mean, how often when listening to someone talking to you do you actually put yourself into the particular scenario that they are talking about? Actually visualise yourself experiencing all of the feelings and actions of the other person, as the story they are portraying unfolds. To me, this is the very essence of "empathy", involving your own senses to heighten the communication process between yourself and someone else.

From a guy's prospective, I have observed a distinct difference between men and women on this very topic. Some time ago I read a great book by Dr Robert Gray called Men Are From Mars, Women Are From Venus it discusses the very obvious differences between men and women (from a psychological prospective not a physical one). And in terms of empathy, men are starting from well behind the blocks. You see, women have a distinct advantage over us blokes, their very nature is to openly discuss with their friends exactly what is on their mind, whereas men tend to be less obvious when sharing their thoughts and particularly their feelings, are more inward with their emotions and defiantly become more withdrawn and retreat into the emotional cave when confronted with an emotional dilemma.

As a consequence of this, women clearly show a heightened ability to express empathy and are generally considered to be more caring than men. I say generally, simply because this activity can be developed and enhanced through effort. Yes that's right, men can change, but there is nothing wrong with a bit of self improvement, particularly when you understand just how important this topic of empathy really is.

Just imagine how (by simply using this technique) much more involved in a conversation with someone you would be if you simply visualise yourself experiencing what it is that they are saying. By involving this additional process, their story becomes so much more meaningful. Let me give you an example.

One of my work colleagues came into my office one day and was quite upset, he then went on to tell me that he was having marriage difficulties and was lost. I asked a series of questions so that I could build an understanding of his situation and the circumstances that had brought him to this point. I will not go into particular details; however, by simply placing myself into his story, I was able to get a sense of how disturbing this problem was. Not only that but I became closer and felt a part of the story. It's like reading a good book, one where as you read it you actually visualise yourself as the main character. So after a very short period of time, I could completely understand just what the problem was, and it was then quite simple to remove myself from this particular issue and look at it holistically and offer the appropriate advice.

It does not have to be such dramatic circumstances where you can apply this, just imagine you're in the sales profession, and someone is outlining their need for a particular goods or service. By simply putting yourself into their story as they deliver it to you, you can get a better feel for their needs. Or what if someone was complaining about a defective product, would you like it if this problem happened to you? The customer can sense if you are genuinely interested in their problem and if you are going to offer assistance or not. By simply choosing to "give a damn" your increased interest will manifest itself in increased sales, increased relationships or increased understanding to no matter what you apply this to. So simple but yet so important. To me that's empathy!

In the introduction I mentioned the relationship of empathy and learning and the education process. As a child growing up in Queensland, I can clearly recall a time in my life when I had no understanding of this concept. Needless to say my results reflected my lack of interest in my surroundings. I just could not get into it. I look back at that time in my life with all of the wisdom and experience that thirty-odd years brings and I shake my head with disbelief that I was once that naïve and how with just a bit of understanding on this topic my education results would have been much different. But you see empathy is not something that is taught at school, well not as far as I was concerned. It is not something that your parents instruct you in. And as mentioned earlier, I think guys are at a disadvantage here.

You see, I was at that time operating on the three "R's": read, remember and repeat. And to make matters worse I can clearly recall one particular history teacher who insisted that we write down all of the lecture notes off the blackboard, so one is only focusing on the copying of the text, in a ridiculous time frame that would result in only a limited amount of the information copied, and in my case was so illegible that it was useless anyway. Now I have subsequently learnt that in fact I have dyslexia and today I would (one would hope) be diagnosed with this learning disability. Now I don't doubt that some may adequately learn in this format, but I certainly did not.

I have subsequently learnt this simple thing. **"It does not matter what words you are hearing or read, it is simply what they mean to you that counts".** Allow your mind to wander and recall a story that relates what you're hearing to something important to you, maybe a past experience or memory that is directly related to this topic. It is very important to separate "daydreaming" from what I am saying here, the thought or feeling must be directly related to the words you are hearing, do not allow your mind to drift off on a different tangent, stay focused and concentrate. It is this association that allows you to lock away this information and in fact involve a different region of your brain. You will have a stronger synaptic connection in your brain that is heightened every time you recall the image or memory, thus improving the recall of the context.

You see I had to learn this process for myself, no one showed it to me. I will admit that the Bob Proctor seminars I went to touched on this point, I found their format was for me, much more conducive to learning.

The format was quite simply one person talking on a stage using visual aids and this presentation being recorded on an audio tape that I would play over and over again. Now I have been to several lectures on many topics, but I have found that if you simply listen to and watch the speaker, observe their body language and mannerisms, allow your mind to relate similar stories to what you are hearing and involve this "feeling" element it actually means more to you. If you then can get a written copy of the course notes for later reference if there is to be an exam on the topic all the better, but I have found if you just focus on the here and now, namely concentrate on the words being said, relate them to your life and your experiences and you will be able to recall the lecture indefinitely. Again to me, that is a form of "empathy". I like to think of it as "empathetic understanding" (well it works for me anyway).

So let's now apply this concept to your life, albeit in enhancing "goal setting" or whatever area you wish to develop. Don't be afraid of attaching feelings and emotion to your everyday life. I believe it leads to a richer and better understanding of life. If you are a manager of people or have staff working under you, try this technique, by applying empathy to your staff several changes will occur and they are all for the better. Firstly by showing that you are actually interested in their particular life and circumstances, you enhance the connection and bond between them and you! So why is this so important? Well quite simply I have seen so many examples of poor management techniques that could be best described as a dictatorship rather then effective management. A good manager is someone who leads by example, and in turn is not afraid of what the staff thinks of them.

During a recent round of staff reviews in our office, this very topic was raised. One of our staff had received a very complementary review and was actually quite uncomfortable about this. When I questioned him about this process and indeed the reasons why he felt uncomfortable, his response took me by surprise, you see he said, from his experience he had been used to working for managers that seem to take pleasure in damaging his self-esteem rather then developing his self-esteem. As he explained the circumstances to me, it almost appeared as if his previous employers enjoyed this method of control like some perverse egomaniac power play! How destructive and how misguided.

Further more, with this particular employee, I have developed a close sense of trust and respect, in that we constantly talk about the development of this book and in turn applying these concepts and ideals to enrich his life. You see to me, this is what it is all about! Helping people to help them self, which is one of the most satisfying aspects of my working life, and in turn contributes to my self-esteem and satisfaction in my career.

A second yet surprisingly similar occurrence took place just last week. This particular example took place while a young work college and I were conducting some energy audits for a series of schools. The objective was to identify the energy usage and identify elements that could lead to reducing the energy consumption and in turn reduce the carbon footprint of the facility. However the reason as to why we were there is not important moreover it was a case that had the opportunity to get to know some one that had only spent a short time with us a sub-contractor. You see for the second time in the one week I was completely surprised to learn the same thing, and that was just how pleasant it was to work in our environment.

From my perspective I enjoyed helping someone who had not come across these ideas before, and by sharing those with her had the opportunity to enrich her life and help her to identify her goals and work towards them.

The second benefit that becomes apparent when you develop a sense of empathy and awareness with your staff is by simply getting to know them, you see what interests them, and by offering further training or developing their interests, they in turn become both better skilled, which in turn helps the profile and productivity of the company, but also they become more motivated and interested in their career. So you see every way you look at it there are benefits everywhere, a real win/win situation.

> **"Teachers open the door, but you enter by yourself."**
>
> *Anonymous*

6 PASSION FOR WHAT IT IS YOU DO

In this chapter we look at just what it is within us, that driving force of motivation from deep within, and how to develop and use this emotion towards what we desire, truly a powerful concept when fully understood. Closely linked to empathy, however, passion comes from within. This chapter will help you better understand your innermost thoughts, your "Sanctum Sanctorum", the me that I see, is the me I will be. We look at your self image and how to improve it by gaining an understanding of yourself.

Passion is an emotional state; just imagine a relationship without passion. Passion is an emotion closely related to love and love is the most powerful energy in the universe. Remember earlier when I talked about energy levels and how love is the polar opposite to hate!

To be passionate about something improves the focus and energy you apply to something. I say something, simply because it can be applied to anything, relationships, career, hobbies, it does not matter what area you think about, by invoking passion the energy level (or the frequency) improves and is increased.

A simple example of this can be observed in a relationship. We all can remember a time when we first fell in love with someone. Now love is a perfectly natural state, and I choose this example because we all have loved at some time. You seem to become so focused on your partner, nothing else seems to matter, you block out any external forces or influences that contrast from this state. You focus only on the relationship, or in other words, you focus only on your goal, not allowing any other influences, affect the outcome.

So you can see where I am going with this, right? The same can be said about your career. I have heard it said that I am very passionate about my profession and industry. Well I am, but this makes it very easy to talk about to others. I sometimes hear myself when talking to a client, not so much the words I am saying but moreover the emotion and passion behind the words. My observations are this: when you talk to someone when you are passionate about the topic (and it does not matter what that topic is) your faith and belief in the subject matter is expressed. Now the person that you are talking to can see this passion, and subconsciously they have no choice but to believe you.

Think of this example as energy levels, remember love is the highest level of energy and energy can only flow from a high state to a lower state. When you talk to someone about something that they are not familiar with, their mind is open, your energy is flowing from you to them. It is impossible to flow the other way, the more energy behind your discussion the faster and stronger your point is received.

Look at the converse situation, you are trying to convey your point without much belief, faith or conviction. As you can imagine your point will not be well received, the person you are talking to may already have their own opinion and belief on the topic and your non-emotional words will have little effect.

When you speak with passion, it is an automatic process: you do it without thought. The person to whom you are talking to will except what you are saying as the truth, with an underlying belief that you must be an expert as you talk with such passion. See my point!

Think about this the next time somebody is explaining something to you, do they really know what they are talking about? Are they passionate about what they are saying and how they say it? Or are they just repeating some propaganda in the hope that someone will believe them?

I am able to derive a successful career in the mechanical services field as a consulting engineer, simply because I have been involved in the same industry for over twenty-five years. It's what I do, my speciality. Now obviously the person I am consulting to simply cannot have the same or more experience in this field, or why would they need my services!

Truth is they will be experienced in their own field, but they have asked for my help on matters relating to air conditioning, ventilation, code compliance or energy minimisation and the like. Now the point I want to stress is this: because I believe in what I am saying, I can invoke empathy and involve the person I am talking to by involving their interest and conveying my discussion in such a way that it means something to them. Their interest is heightened, simply because I am giving them the scientific reasons addressing their complaint and providing the solution to eliminate the source of complaint. They develop an understanding in the nature of their problem, while at the same time developing a respect for me and my knowledge. And believe me, when you make a living as a consultant, this respect is important. My confidence is delivered subliminally within my words and actions i.e. my body language. Because my confidence is high, the energy behind my message is high. This energy flows from me to the subject quickly and easily, and in most cases my point is well received.

Just imagine the same scenario, but this time imagine that the conversation is being delivered by someone who does not really understand the nature of the problem, they are just making it up, or have no or little understanding themself. The outcome will be very different, simply because the energy levels are much less. The recipient of the information will quickly discern that they are being told a load of rubbish and the credibility is not established, the true nature of the problem won't be addressed thus further reducing the credibility of the so-called "expert".

No doubt you can relate this example to what it is you do, or you may have been the recipient of some ill-informed advice. But you can see how by involving passion, your message and therefore your credibility is enhanced.

If you're in a sales career, you know that you first must believe in and fully understand the nature of your product. For if you do not, you will be very quickly revealed as a fake. Not only will you blow the sale, but more importantly, you will damage your credibility.

Become an expert in your field and the rest will follow. Think of how many successful sales people or providers of a service or advice have actually changed their career, and ended up deriving an income from a field that was their hobby. They are interested in this field, they enjoy what they do and therefore they do it very well. This confidence is expressed every time they talk about it and the circle is continued! You see, it is natural to involve passion when you are excited or believe in something, it is not so easy to involve passion when you are not motivated or interested, and human nature is such that your lack of interest will quickly be observed and the outcome will not be as positive and successful as you had intended.

My good friend, mentor and business partner Brad Maynard and I were discussing this very point the other day. A client of ours was asking Brad just what it is that we, in our consulting business, do differently to other firms. Brad answered, "it is quite simple, the three directors of the firm are all 'fridgies'", i.e. all from the trade with a refrigeration, commissioning or air-conditioning background.

Naturally everything that I have discussed above is automatic for everyone in our firm, our clients get the results they are looking for, but not only that, there are those in our industry who do not have the same level of experience and unintentionally deliver the wrong outcome with limited results.

We are truly blessed in that not only are the three directors of our firm passionate about what we do, but this then filters down to each of the employees.

Combine this with an active succession plan, namely most of our employees actually are shareholders of the company, then you have a truly successful formula, involving a group of people who are motivated and united in the common good of the firm. Recall a previous comment, that there are only two ways of making money:

    1. Money working for you.
    2. People working for you.

Then as you can see here, we truly have a successful model in place, because as a collective each individual is actually benefitting from the wealth of experience of those around them. And it is a two way street, my knowledge is enhanced by others in the firm due to their past experiences and expertise, as I know my knowledge is flowing to my associates.

Fall in love with what you do, your passion will instantly and automatically take over and you will be successful, I am certain of it!

It is one thing that is so predictable and repeatable, it should be a "law of the universe".

> **"If we each selfishly pursue only what we believe to be in our own interest, without caring about the need of others, we not only end up harming others but also ourselves."**
>
> *The Dalai Lama*

7 I.Q. vs E.Q.

In this chapter we look at the relationship between I.Q. (Intelligence Quota) and E.Q. (Emotional Quota) or emotional intelligence. Most who read this may not have heard the term "E.Q." before, in fact I only heard the term a few years ago myself. Emotional Quota is just that, the amount of emotion and emotional development you have been exposed to in your life. Your emotional experience. As such it is continuously evolving and improving throughout life's journey.

Whereas I.Q. is your reasoning ability, the way your brain solves problems and as such is traditionally more fixed and difficult to change.

So to better explain this point, we need to understand the comparative discussed in this chapter, namely "I.Q.". Like most, as a school student, I participated in an I.Q. test. This test, as the name suggests, is used to determine the intelligence of a person; however, the particular test I remember undertaking was focusing on the particular direction a school leaver would be best suited to. As I recall, my results suggested a slightly above average intelligence and that I should pursue a career in the sales and engineering field. At that time I did not understand the importance of what was being explained to me, after all how could I possibly believe that I was above average intelligence, when in reality my grades did not suggest anything of the sort?

I have since come to realise that it is possible to identify one's personality trait, and typically we can be categorised into seven fundamental personalities. My understanding of this point has evolved as a result of the social interactivity that has occurred over the years. However the point that I want to make is this: our Intelligence Quota is pretty much a fixed quantity, largely determined at birth. Now I truly believe it is possible to change one's personality, especially if you have understood all of the topics as previously discussed in this book at least. Your personality is a function of your thoughts, feelings and actions. However my point here is that I.Q. alone I believe accounts for very little.

Some years ago, I saw a wonderful documentary and the subject matter was entitled *Emotional Intelligence*. The timing of the documentary was brilliant in that I had been asked to speak at the Regency Park TAFE Graduation dinner with an anticipated audience of 350 people. I already knew that my talk was to look at my experiences at the TAFE some twenty years earlier, and my journey that lead me to be the director of a consulting firm and director of a not for profit industry institute. The documentary looked at several successful Australian business people, one of whom was John Ilhan or better known as "Crazy John" the phone company founder (who sadly passed away not long after this particular interview). The documentary also interviewed several other personalities, and one clear trend was obvious. Each of the successful business people all spoke of "Emotional Intelligence".

Each of the personalities understood that your I.Q. was no where near as important as your E.Q. You see in order to be successful in business you must have faith in your abilities, this faith is based on your experiences up to that point in time, and the belief in yourself. I then thought about what I was hearing and then applied empathy to the story. You see, I too had a time of running my own business when things were not going so well, when my goals and outcome were very different than my current mindset. But the fundamental essence of this documentary was the point that each of the interviewed had this very understanding. It does not matter what your I.Q. is, what matters is your vision, your belief in yourself and how you apply yourself, that defines us. Now remember this point: it is the sum of your experiences both **good** and **bad** that is your Emotional Intelligence.

Combine this concept with your goal, vision or faith. This is what I believe is the essence of Emotional Intelligence.

So how can we apply our new understanding of this fundamental point? Well I believe it is a simple as this: now that we have defined it, we can now understand it, and when you understand something, the fear surrounding the subject disappears. Fear is replaced with knowledge and understanding. This is the very essence of awareness and awareness overcomes its polar opposite – ignorance. It is the sum of all your experiences combined with your beliefs and goals that is your Emotional Intelligence, and that is what separates the ordinary from the extraordinary, and the winners from those that have not yet reached this level of intellectual understanding.

From this you should now be able to see that it is OK to have failed at something. As long as you have learnt from the experience, you can then draw from this experience and ensure it does not happen again.

Now this concept is not limited to business, it is equally true for everything: relationships, education, even our life journey can be enriched by this understanding.

Don't be afraid of failing, or failure. Use failure as a learning experience. Learn to look back at failure with this new understanding, realise that it has made you who you are up to this point, but that is in the past. If you learn from past mistakes you can see when a change in direction is required in order to not repeat the same action.

Remember the earlier chapter "Looking at life in the rear vision mirror"? If we can learn from our past mistakes and make sure they are not repeated, then our journey is heading in a different direction and the same outcome will not eventuate. The future is "unwritten", we create our own destiny and future as we go along, it is purely the choices we make along the way that determine our outcome, not our past results. The understanding of this point is "**Emotional Intelligence**".

From a different perspective, but one I believe is closely related, is your "self-esteem". I am currently reading a powerful book by Nathaniel Branden entitled *The Six Pillars of Self-Esteem*, where similar conclusions are discussed but the author focuses on self-esteem. Highlighting the fact that your self-esteem is a result of your past experience, he further defines some of the psychological issues resulting from an unhealthy self-esteem. Again by applying empathy, I can easily relate this understanding to some of the decisions

I have made, and furthermore, understand some of the apparently illogical decisions made by myself and others in my life.

Throughout my life I have seen it as one of my responsibilities to help those around me; I have accounted some of these examples in this book. However in order to understand and offer advice you must first understand the mind-set of the person you are talking to. I have found that having an understanding of this chapter can be used to increase the understanding of the complexities that are our life experiences. Here is an interesting example. Re-read this chapter (go on, it is only a few pages) and apply it to your own life, or even try and relate it to someone who you think would benefit from this knowledge.

I have said it many times throughout this book, that happiness is the true measure of our success. It is my underlying motivation to not only increase the happiness in my life, but the happiness of those around me. The concept in this chapter may be new to most who read these words, but I firmly believe when fully understood they will make a world of difference in improving one's self-image, self-esteem and self-worth and this is where it all starts.

Following on from the previous chapter, and now involving an understanding of emotional intelligence,

I have observed that people can be broken up into two categories:

- Those that are easily influenced simply because they have little or no Emotional Intelligence, or street smarts. They tend to believe pretty much anything they are told, and as such go through life on the path of least resistance. Always looking for an easy way to make a dollar, a get rich scheme or unfounded belief that they will win the Lotto. They always tend to come second at everything, and always tend to end up with more of the same. (Remember the chapter on vibration and attraction). They have no commitment to completion, may pick up a book such as this one, but not have the conviction to complete reading it.

- Or the second category, someone who has developed Emotional Intelligence, who has developed a wisdom that tends to come with life experiences. This person will not be so easily influenced, as they can habitually and instantly discern between fact and fiction. And in the case of reading a book like this, will not only finish it but actually re-read it a few times and have empathy for the content and have the ability to learn, use and grow from the content.

By now I truly hope that you can see that if you fall into the first category, that is OK but understand you can change. Learn from your mistakes, develop an understanding that by implementing the concepts discussed in this book you can change your life.

While my main focus has been to talk about happiness, these concepts can be implemented to achieve anything. I can recall hearing a saying some years ago, and that is: **anything the mind can conceive it can achieve!**

The trouble is for most of us we don't know what we want, or if you do actually conceive an original idea you may lack the understanding it takes to develop your idea to realise its full potential.

One final point on Emotional Intelligence, by now you should be able to see that E.Q. is indeed something that can be learned and improved just as any other skill set. One sure method to improve your knowledge base is to read! Read anything you can get your hands on. This book may be the first self help book that you have read, but believe me when you develop a thirst for knowledge reading self help books can deliver a vast and wide source of information, I like reading particularly last thing at night when I go to bed, I find it gives me the ability to switch off from the days activities and immerse myself into a world of knowledge. You get to choose the subject matter and read at your own pace, if you at first do not fully understand the concept, re-read it again and again until you fully understand, then you can move on.

It makes sense that if E.Q. is the sum of all of the tactile experiences; conversation you have had or been a part of, then reading books such as this one will contribute to your data bank of knowledge. The more information contained with-in your data bank the higher the wealth of knowledge you draw from when confronted with a new situation or a circumstance that requires your intellectual input. The more you read, the faster and fluent you become at it.

One measure of success that I have developed is by taking pride and developing my own library of books and other reading material, this is both on self help and motivation, but also on my other interests such as wine and personal fitness. To be well read is to be well informed, and it is something that is so simple to implement and learn from. I derive great satisfaction at looking at my bookshelf and knowing that I have read every word of every book or magazine on display. I will admit that this is a work in progress, like my wine collection, but both bring me satisfaction and this in turn contributes to my own happiness.

This can also include books on successful people you admire, from my perspective autobiographies are a great tool to gain understanding as to what sets those that are successful and extraordinary from the ordinary.

This is how I have come to learn about Emotional Intelligence, a subject that should be more widely understood.

> **"While one person hesitates because he feels inferior, the other is busy making mistakes and becoming superior."**
>
> Henry C. Link

8 SPIRITUALITY

Spirituality is such a misunderstood word, in that it is often associated with religion (well at least I used to make that connection). It is important to separate the two in order to understand the context in which I wish to discuss. For some, spirituality is directly related to religion, but as I may have alluded to earlier, I have never really had much faith in any one particular religion.

But the key words here are **faith** and **spirituality** and they don't necessarily need to be associated in a religious connotation. It is my belief that faith in one's self is far more important than the belief in a conventional religion. Having said that, I express my own opinion, if you are able to maintain a faith in a religious sense, I commend you, however for me I have never really been attracted to one religion over another.

My definition of faith is simply: **The belief in the impossible, and the ability to see the invisible, to achieve the incredible.** This can simply be expressed as a creative process; it does not bind you to any one religion!

Having said that, I still would class myself as a spiritual person, in that my belief is focused on me and my abilities and my contributions to humanity, with my spiritual journey simply being the quest to better and further understand my own mind. My hope is that if you have actually read this book up to this point, you should be able to see that I consider myself to be a person of high moral standing, and I have said earlier that I believe it is my responsibility to help those around me, particularly if they seek my help. Furthermore to be an active member of your local community (to actually contribute and not be a burden) is also part of the big picture.

So I am talking about faith in one's self. I think it is important to be able to see yourself as a spiritual being and to gain an understanding of the link between fulfilment and happiness.

Some years ago I was fortunate to see the following diagram, and as simple as it is, I use it often in conversation with people as it allows us to see the various elements of our life.

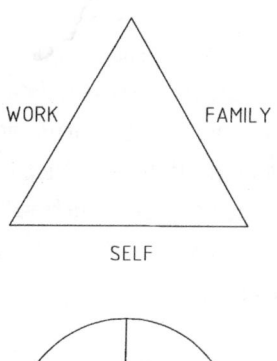

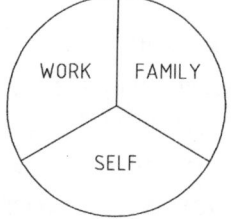

The three key life elements

Put very simply, there are three main elements in your life: **yourself**, your **family** and family commitments, and your work or **career**. I truly think that most of us go through life putting our predominant thoughts and energy to the work and family side, and tending to forget ourselves!

The trouble is, if you forget about yourself for long enough you forget to do the things that you love to do, the things that actually make you happy, and it is these things that define your spirituality!

Consider this as a circular process: if each element is not fulfilled then the other two areas (family and work) will subconsciously suffer. For it is my opinion that only when all three elements are operating in a fully symbiotic way that true happiness is achieved. Moreover, I also believe that until the "self" component is satisfied and content, then the other two elements can not be fulfilled.

I actually like that the "self" component is on the base or bottom, as I consider this element to be the most fundamental and important. This is certainly the case with love and relationships. How many times have you heard the saying, "you can't love someone else until you love yourself"? Well the very ideal I am talking about here is an extension of this concept. In that the "self" component is made up of self-esteem, self-respect and self-belief which have been summarised previously in this book.

So how do you improve the "self" part?

Firstly you need to understand the importance of the triangle and that it is OK to consider your happiness in order to complete the fulfilment of life. For me it was as simple as immersing myself in physical fitness and physical activities, by trying as many experiences as I possibly could, and finding out what I like to do, as well as if I enjoyed it or it made me feel happy, I would simply do more of that.

The trick is to try everything once, if you don't like it, don't do it again. But you will find that there are many things that put that silly grin on your face and are inexpensive activities such as mountain bike riding (as a matter of fact, I am off for a ride as soon as I write this paragraph).

In my life I have been fortunate enough to fly aeroplanes, drive nice cars, and enjoy riding my jet-ski, but the thing here is to find out what **you** like to do, and simply do more of that. By simply planning then doing something that you have wanted to do for ages, but never got around to doing, this simple step forward will result in increasing your happiness, and you never know, you might actually have some fun along the way!

Push the envelope, get out of your comfort zone, and try new things.

> **"Too much of a good thing can be wonderful."**
>
> *Mae West*

By extension of this concept, if you can find activities that involve your family, then you can work on two of the key life elements at the same time. For example, I know my girls love riding with me on my jet-ski, particularly my middle daughter who seems to take as much delight from me trying to throw her off as I get out of it, and wave jumping, measuring the "air time" by the distance of the break in the wake! Extreme fun!

Take your family out for a picnic, or go bush walking together, like I said these are inexpensive activities, but the important thing is to get out, be active and enjoy each other's company.

Now it is not my intention to gloss over the importance of the other two elements, "work" and "family", but I am going to assume that you already know that everything we have looked at here is valid and relevant in these two areas as well.

You should aim to derive satisfaction from your work, but to define what it is that gives us satisfaction is a truly unique thing, and it is not my intention to write about the complexities that go into defining a career! Other than to say, motivation comes from within, you first want to be motivated towards a goal or result in order to receive motivation or "direction" from someone else. No doubt you have heard the old saying: "**you can lead a horse to water, but you can't make it drink!**"

The same can be said for "family". This is also "unique

to your situation", but understand this; you must continuously evaluate and assess each element of your life as you go along, take accountability and responsibility for each element as you go, for you are in control of your destiny, you and you alone shape your future!

Life is truly a fluid concept, continuously changing and evolving, and unless you continually take stock of where you are at, what your are doing, and how you plan to get to where you are going, understand that habitual thinking and old conditioning creep in and you can easily slip back into the comfort zone, and as I said earlier, the comfort zone is a bad place to be!

Make a conscious choice to be the best person you can be, and work at that every day. Sounds simple I know, but it is truly as simple as making that choice and acting out that plan!

A classic mistake I often see is in the case of women that are trying to balance a family life with a career and in many cases seem to forget their own importance. The "self" component is the last on the list, or the first to miss out. But the key word is "balance". Understand the importance of this concept, that your life is not sustainable unless you give appropriate attention to each of the three key elements. By sustainable, I mean that with enough neglect something has to give, and it is usually your own happiness and spirituality.

Again I don't wish to stereotype and each person's circumstances are unique, but unless you understand the importance of the three key elements and their relationship to each other, then you run the risk of directing your energy and efforts into the two other areas and the only loser in this situation is your happiness and your fulfilment of life itself. A classic symptom of this problem is an unhappy partner, and by extension of this, their sex life is lacking and unfulfilled. But to me a couple's sex life is an excellent gauge or barometer of the health of the relationship.

The male partner is grumpy that there is "no loving" going on, and it is the last thing on the female's mind, and before too long resentment creeps in, emotions grow in a negative direction and ultimately the relationship breaks down.

Unfortunately I have seen this unfold for myself, and like I said I do not wish to generalise, but I am speaking here from personal experience. Looking back with the benefit of hindsight, communication in the relationship is paramount, if one partner is too dopey to see all of the telltale signs that there is a problem, then tell them! **"A problem shared is a problem halved."**

I have subsequently devised a simple test or barometer that can be used to determine the health of your relationship; it can also be used to determine your satisfaction in pretty much any area, career and the like. And that is simply think of a line, with good on the top and bad on the bottom. As time goes along adjust how much time is spent above the line or below the line. If there is more time (i.e. greater then 50 percent) in the plus side or above the line, well that's good, but if the majority of time is below the line, well that's not so good, and obviously something needs to change, for continuation along this path will result in failure, dissatisfaction or unhappiness.

But understand this, life is full of ups and downs but it is the predominate state that counts. Remember earlier in this book we looked at the concept of the predominate state of your thoughts, and how the law of attraction states that you attract into your life what you think about the most. Well I put it to you now that if your predominate thought or even predominate state is below the line in an unhappy existence, well you will only perpetuate more of the same, and you will attract more of the same, but that's how it works, for both good and bad! But also understand this, you can change, you can choose to change, these are not just words here, this is all about the understanding that you are in control of your life, for if you are not in control, then who is?

EMOTIONAL STATE

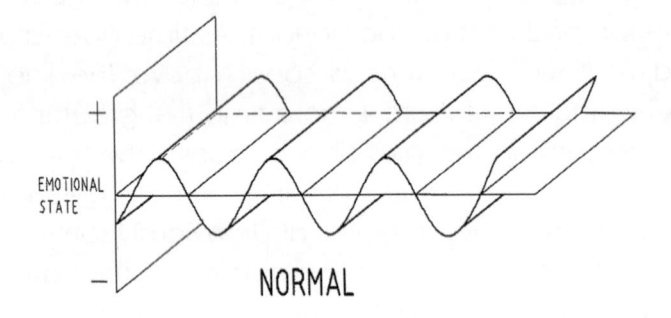

NORMAL

In this diagram, the normal state of emotional variations is depicted; they may not be as regular as shown here (or follow such an even frequency) but the point is that it is perfectly normal for your mood and therefore your emotional state to go through its ups and downs.

GENERALLY OPTOMISTIC STATE

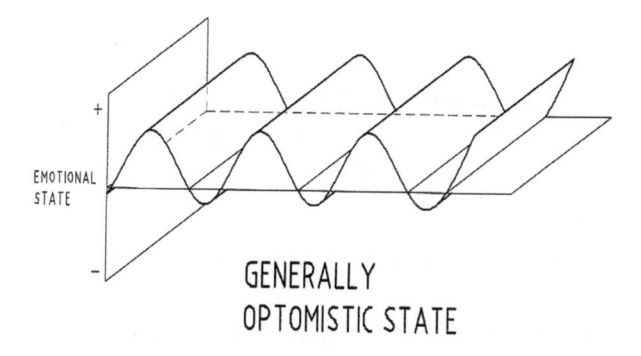

In this diagram a generally optimistic outlook is depicted. I believe this would best depict my emotional state, in that I am able to control my emotional state by choosing my thoughts and implementing all of the concepts described in this book.

This is not to say that I never suffer un-happiness or am consciously aware that I am in a negative vibration, it is more that I am aware I can control this and there for change it (unless of course it is Monday morning and the kids are less then enthusiastic about getting ready for school and a mad panic ensues).

I also believe that with a higher level of awareness and understanding it is possible to even out the peaks and troughs, just imagine what a Tibetan monk's emotional state would look like with such devotion to meditation and prayer. However that's not for me, and I am happy with my current state.

EMOTIONAL STATE

DEPRESSION

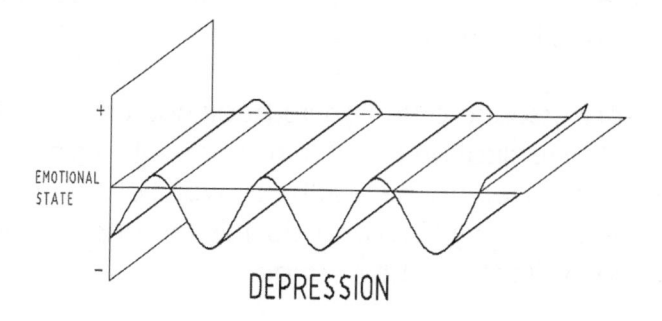

This third emotion state of depression or prolonged sadness is as a result of life circumstances being out of control. And again I do not wish to generalise, but I am of the opinion that someone who is generally unhappy can and does get quite comfortable about being in a negative vibration, because this is there normal emotional state for the majority of time, they become complaisant and comfortable in this state.

I would go so far as to say, when they pop above the normal line, they actually feel quite uncomfortable about being happy as this is not a normal thing for them to experience, so their sub-conscious mind does what it can to bring them back to a comfortable state, i.e. unhappiness.

The very essence of this entire book has led us to this point, the realisation that if things are not so good, or you are not getting the results you want, change your thoughts and thinking and do this for long enough and you will attract the change.

In the case of the relationship issues touched on earlier, if you trace the root of the problem you inevitably find the source is due to lack of understanding of the three key elements, in that the "self" component gets neglected. In turn your self-esteem and self-worth take a hit, and if this continues for long enough you end up living a compromised life. To continue without change is ignorance, but how often do we just keep going on, thinking/wishing/hoping one day we will be rescued from this self-imprisonment?

Understand that the answer lies within, you alone hold the key to your destiny. By changing your thoughts, visualising yourself living the lifestyle you want, continually evaluating your life as you go along to make sure you are not letting the past results or mistakes control your journey, and develop the understanding that true fulfilment can only be achieved when all three of the key life elements are complete, then you are on the right track, and as I put it you have achieved **"spiritual enlightenment"**. That's right, in my opinion the elusive life pursuit of spiritual enlightenment is as simple as mastering this very ideal and concept. Living a joyful and fulfilled life is our birthright and I believe it is something we work on everyday!

> **"Life has a bright side and a dark side,
> for the world of relativity
> is composed of light and shadows.
> If you permit your thoughts to dwell on evil,
> you yourself will become ugly.
> Look only for the good in everything,
> that you absorb the quality of beauty."**
>
> *Paramshansa Yognada*

9 YOUR HEALTH IS YOUR WEALTH

There are so many benefits from both a physical and psychological perspective when you increase your physical activities in the pursuit of enjoyment and happiness.

Using my own personal experience here as an example, as I look back at the past four years my growth in this area has been dramatic. By applying the concepts that I have discussed in this book, I am now a truly different and better person than I was some years ago. From a physical perspective all of the activities such as bike riding, working out in my home gym and my love for swimming have all culminated in a physical package that I now am satisfied with (well almost satisfied with).

So what do I mean by "satisfied with"? Well it is as simple as looking in the mirror! Are you happy with the way you look? Now I know that most people will say no, but if you are one of the very few who could actually say "yes" – good on you! Well done! But for most this is not the case.

I believe that your physical appearance and particularly your **perception** of your appearance is a large contributor to most people's unhappiness. If you recall I discussed this point in the first chapter, in my case it takes anywhere from eight to ten hours a week exercising to achieve my desired appearance, but I actually enjoy doing it. And when you enjoy doing something it is not a chore or a task to do it.

In my case, I know the physical fitness allows me to deal with the stresses and pressures life throws at me, but this is all part of the balanced approach, this in turn leads to developing a satisfied self-esteem and self-worth. Not to mention the increased longevity having a healthy and active lifestyle can bring.

It is my belief that our body is simply a vessel which supports our spirit, and by that I believe the spirit is the mind. When the vessel is no longer able to support the mind and associated mind/brain functions such as memories, dreams and the like, at the time of death the spirit or energy leaves the body and travels throughout the universe in the form of energy.

That's my belief, but doesn't it make sense to actually make your body (the vessel) as efficient as possible? I truly think that most people do not understand that we are here for one shot at this game of life, this is not a practice run – we only get one shot!

By extension of this theory, don't you think we should invest time and effort into the state and condition of our body, with the understanding that both the mind and body also share a symbiotic relationship – what happens to one will affect the other!

Healthy thinking, combined with a healthy lifestyle, made up of the right balance of physical activity and the right choices in your diet are what we control, no one is forcing you to eat junk or food high in saturated fats and the like, modern lifestyle and complacency have led to some pretty unhealthy choices for most. But understand that a balanced approach is required.

Take an interest in your health! Learn more about the importance of food, and the effect on your body, your energy levels and your ability to perform day to day tasks. Let me give you an example. My diet has been anything but perfect, but after years of reading health magazines such as Men's Health (and I must confess I was only reading out of interest in the physical exercise stories) I started to understand the relationship between getting the best out of my body by choosing what I put into it!

Now it is not just the relationship between physical performance here, I have discovered through my reading and research the relationship between

Omega 3 and our brain activity. Up until recently my diet was not rich in seafood, so I was not eating a natural or normal quantity of fish oil /Omega 3. I then read many articles in *Men's Health* about the benefits Omega 3 brings to brain activity by improving the brain's ability to perform the synaptic electrical impulse that is a thought. So I decided to start taking Omega 3 supplements. At first the quantity was quite low, and I must admit there was no real noticeable benefit, so I increased the amount to levels advised by my doctor (more about that later). But needless to say, upon reflection, there was an enormous change over a period of time and one that draws similarities to the following.

A year or two later, I purchased a copy of the BBC documentary *The Human Mind* and to my surprise it tells the story of a survey conducted on several school children in England. Typically before the trial most children had some form of learning difficulty, or were just the result of today's "couch potato" lifestyle.

The children then took six tablets a day for three months. The results were outstanding, and in the case of one particular boy at the centre of the article, he went from being a below average student to a compulsive reader. The article concludes with his comment that he now considers the library to be his favourite place! What a dramatic change and one that I had empathy for given my own noticeable changes. My memory and ability to recall information was enhanced, but for me the most apparent improvement was the ability to focus and concentrate. I would go so far as to say that four years ago I would never have considered writing a book such as this, yet here I am typing these words on my laptop waiting for my kids to wake up so we can have bacon and eggs for breakfast.

I guess what I am saying here is that in life there is not one silver bullet, no quick fix or magic pill that you can take and hey presto you're a genius. Instead there are several factors and the complexities are unique to each of us. But understand this, there is a relationship between a healthy mind and a healthy body, and when the two are working in harmony and are at their peek efficiency, then I believe you are on the right track.

One final story about my journey and why I have put so much importance into this topic.

About seven years ago my father passed away at the age of sixty-two from bowl cancer. Now this, as you can imagine, was a terrible time for me and my family, with my mother being left a widow at the age of just sixty. Death is at any time an unpleasant reality of life's journey, but my father was only sixty-two. In the months and years since I have reflected on life, and this reflection has led me to an appreciation of life. As I have mentioned I have three beautiful daughters and combined with living a very rich and satisfied life, I have no intention of leaving this mortal soil prematurely. I know there are no certainties here, when your number's up, it's up. But it is my belief that we can make both our minds and bodies as efficient as they are meant to be! And with this efficiency comes (hopefully) greater life expectancy!

Am I over-compensating in my obsession with physical fitness and appearance? I think not. I am driven to achieve a certain look, but the look is to me the physical manifestation of a healthy body operating at an efficient and one could say perfectly natural state.

I will never forget the time as I approached forty; I underwent a series of medical exams ranging from the usual cholesterol levels, LDLs, HDLs, triglycerides and the like. Now at that particular time, my lifestyle was not as it is today. I will never forget being told by my doctor that my cholesterol levels were too high, and blood pressure was too high, etc, etc! I remember being handed a pamphlet on "living with diabetes" and thinking, no way! This is not for me!

This event, combined with the passing of my father,

literally shocked me into action! I immersed myself in studying nutrition, I bought a mountain bike and over the following years developed the lifestyle that I now live today. So from a physical perspective, I am trying to make this body of mine as efficient as I can, but what I am surprised about has been the enjoyment and satisfaction I continually derive from it, in particular the measurable improvements that allow us to push ourselves further and harder. I can recall the exhilaration after riding up a relatively small hill and completing a 30km ride. This last weekend a mate of mine and I rode up Mt Lofty (the largest hill in South Australia, around 3300 feet or just over 1000 metres). So I am continuously amazed at the body's ability to improve and adapt, and now invite the challenge of a 80–100km ride!

The moral to this particular story, I am pleased to say, is a very different set of results. About a year ago I was re-tested for all of the same things, and I am pleased to report that everything is normal, with a low cholesterol level, excellent blood pressure levels, and my most pleasing result was my doctor turning to me and saying, "Wow, that's one of the biggest changes I have seen, how did you do that?" I know the journey that I am currently on is the right one. But understand the analogy that life and lifestyles are a journey, and every now and then we need to take stock, re-evaluate, and re-set our thinking and habitual choices that make up our life!

Understand the importance of your mental health, and the correlation between self-esteem and self-image to create your spirituality or mind-set, and when you combine this with the physical body, you have a healthy mind and healthy body.

I hope by now you can see that your personal wealth and money or lack thereof, should not be your predominant thought! Instead your health and happiness should be!

Your health is truly your wealth!

For it is my belief that when you get this part right, the rest will follow and you can have anything you desire! Bob Proctor once said "**Abundance is our birthright**". Some use this knowledge for financial gain, and you certainly can do that, but it is my intention to help you develop your happiness and wellness that is our birthright, for once you get that part right, the rest will follow.

10 APPLICATION

It is my intention in this chapter to not raise any new ideas or concepts, but rather to bring conclusion to all of the concepts and universal laws we have looked at throughout this book. As no doubt there have been some elements discussed that were possibly quite foreign to you, so let's re-cap on some of the major concepts:

Firstly we looked at "**accountability**" in the chapter **It all starts with you**. Do you accept the fact that you and you alone have been responsible for all of the decisions that you have made throughout your life? I hope you automatically answer "yes", if not go back and re-read the chapter on accountability. To take responsibility for your own actions and mistakes is all part of growing up. Think of it as emotional growth rather than growing older.

We looked at the "comfort zone" and how it can be a bad place to be. Bad simply because with old conditioning and habitual thinking you just end up with more of the same thing, and for some this is a life of doubt, debt and worry.

Understand the fact that it is up to you to improve your lot in life, be it in a spiritual journey or financial growth, it all starts with and finishes with you! By taking responsibility for your actions allows us to grow and move on.

In the second chapter we looked at **Looking at life through the rear vision mirror**, simply to develop the analogy of accountability and responsibility, by providing the analogy of driving a car and only looking in the rear vision mirror. Without looking forward or having a destination in mind, your journey will be short-lived and you will ultimately crash!

Life is a journey, start each day with meaning, you must establish goals in life, have a purpose, embrace life, live and love for we only get one shot at it.

An interesting footnote to Marc's story: it has been around two years since I wrote that part of this book and if you recall Marc had relocated to Tasmania to hug trees. Well there must only be a certain amount of trees one can hug, because I am pleased to say Marc is returning to work with me again. But what is the real message here has been his own story of personal development and spiritual growth. The realisation that the grass is not always greener on the other side of the hill and that you take with you the psychological baggage that is you! Simply by moving to a new location will not bring you happiness, happiness comes from within. What an important message and one that is prudent and relevant to establish this very topic!

So the first two chapters of this book are intended to establish the fact that your journey thus far is a result of all of the decisions you have made up to that point, and to establish the realisation that if your life is only going in circles it is simply because of the habitual thinking and focusing on the past that is resulting in more of the same.

Chapter three, the big one, **The universal law of vibration and attraction**.

We develop the understanding that we are all symbiotically connected to the universe and the universe to us, and that our actions have consequences.

Perhaps the most important element of this chapter is the thought process. The link between thoughts being energy and that energy flows from a high source to a low source, and that this is a **"law of the universe"** and you can't change it. When you think a thought, energy will flow from your brain/body/spirit out into the universe.

The universal law of vibration and attraction will ensure that you receive that which you think about the most, so your predominate thoughts had better be good or positive because that's what you attract to your life.

Chapter four looked at **Visualisation to develop goal setting**. Now you can see just how unlimited this concept is, goal setting can be used for so many things, your income, your happiness, acquiring a new car, house, anything. The techniques discussed here allow you to visualise your future and take steps to achieve your dreams.

If the only thing that you take away from this book is the ability to establish new habits and habitual thinking by the use of a goal card, and actually see/visualise yourself in position of your goal/dream. This concept can even be used to change an unhealthy habit such as smoking. This new idea will open up a new world of possibilities to you, I know it works because I have used this technique many times in the past to achieve various goals throughout my life. Now you can too.

Then we looked at **Empathy**. Perhaps this is one area that I believe makes me different from the majority of people, the use and application of empathy can only result in more understanding and "caring" and in today's world surely that must be a good thing!

We looked at how the simple art of conversation is enhanced by the use of empathy: it improves the communication process and enhances learning. Not only that but I think it actually helps improve the quality of life and the quality of person you are.

Following on from empathy is the subject of **Passion**, closely linked, but passion is really empathy from within, directed to you and your life. Think about the good decisions and achievements you have made in your own life, and I am fairly confident that passion, application and commitment to completion have played a significant part in this achievement.

Passion and empathy both help to improve the art of conversation and communication, this in turn improves the quality of our lives and others around us. It enhances our relationships with our partners and our children. Only good things can come from an increased understanding and application of passion and empathy.

So deliberately the first half of this book has been devoted to provide insight into your understanding of you, by establishing the link between thinking, feelings and actions, you can see the relationship between your thoughts and the outcome or results up to this point in time.

The second half of the book is devoted to establishing the understanding that no matter where you are or what you have done up to this point, you can change and improve the quality of your life. The chapter on **I.Q. vs E.Q** introduces us to the power of Emotional Intelligence, to develop the understanding that we learn from our mistakes, and that our Emotional Intelligence is the product or the sum of every decision, thought and conversation that we have had up to that point in our life. It is ever changing and constantly evolving, resulting in the wisdom that comes with age and experience.

The final two chapters, **Spirituality** and **Your health is your wealth** are also closely related, in that we look at the symbiotic relationship between a healthy mind and body. Understanding that they are both related and what happens to one must affect the other. Don't be afraid to think about yourself as a spiritual being occupying your body and your body in turn supporting your life force/spirit, so make your body as efficient as you can, in the hope and pursuit of longevity and the pursuit of happiness.

When you combine all of these concepts together, you can see that we truly are in control of our destiny, we choose the life we want, make each day count and choose to make our life rich with joy and fulfilment! Choose to be the very best that you can be!

Throughout this book I have mentioned some of my favourite sayings that I have picked up along the way and share these with you. This reminds me that none of the ideas contained within this book are mine, no one person can lay claim to them, simply because they have been around for generations. I am truly grateful and remain thankful that I have been lucky enough to be exposed to these ideas and concepts and hope that your life can be enriched by them as well.

I think the following four sayings sum up the essence of this book, and indeed summarise my belief in the potential of human nature and the potential for the good of humankind!

> *"All that we are is a result of what we have thought."*

"It is what we do in the face of adversity or when things go wrong (and they will) that defines who we are!"

*"You create your own
universe as you go along."*

*"Let us not look back in anger,
nor look forward in fear,
but look around us
with awareness!"*

Finally, I can clearly recall the words of my father, who had a favourite saying which was "today is the first day of the rest of your life". Now admittedly this did not mean too much to me many years ago, but I now know this to mean "begin each day with meaning", as each day we begin with a blank page, a fresh sheet of paper. We can either allow the influences of yesterday to effect the new day, or we can choose to start the new day with new hope and new beginning and move forward in a positive direction to achieve our goals and dreams!

ACKNOWLEDGEMENTS

I would like to express my gratitude to the following people for their help and guidance throughout my life journey. My life has been touched and blessed by so many people along the way. Many have been mentioned in the book however the following few have touched me deeply:

Firstly to my friend, mentor and business partner **Mr Brad Maynard**, whose guidance over the last ten years has helped me to become the professional in the consulting engineering field that I am today (my day job and what allows me to pay the bills) and more importantly has shown me/allowed me to become responsible for the training/motivation of our staff, which has in turn given me so much satisfaction and fulfilment in my career.

Secondly, to the man whose vision led me to the ideals contained within this book, and started me on this journey, **Mr Tony Keynes.** And to a man that I have never met, yet has been so central to providing the key to unlocking my potential, **Mr Bob Proctor**.

My three beautiful daughters: **Teagan**, **Shauna** and **Georgia**, who continuously remind me what life is all about and keep me grounded, but also complete me by enriching my life for it is them who inspire me to strive to be a better person and build a legacy!

My mother, **Betty** for her continuing support. I know my father would have been proud of what I am trying to achieve here. It is truly my wish to help others by discussing the ideals that have helped me.

To my work colleague **Ms Fiona Forbes** whose skills in word processing have helped me supplement my own deficiencies in writing these words.

And finally to **you** for taking the time to read this book, I hope that it has provided some insight to help you on your journey through life.

Thank you!

ORDER

It all starts with you!
by Kevin O'Reilly

ISBN 9781921596001   Qty

RRP   AU $24.99   ....

Postage AU $ 5.00   ....

TOTAL* $_____

* All prices include GST

Name: ....

Address: ....

Phone: ....

Email Address: ....

Payment:

❏ Money Order ❏ Cheque ❏ Amex ❏ MasterCard ❏ Visa

Cardholder's Name:..

Credit Card Number: ....

Signature:..

Expiry Date: ....

Allow 21 days for delivery.

Payment to: Better Bookshop (ABN 14 067 257 390)
PO Box 12544
A'Beckett Street, Melbourne, 8006
Victoria, Australia
Fax: +61 3 9671 4730
betterbookshop@brolgapublishing.com.au

BE PUBLISHED

Publishing through a successful Australian publisher. Brolga provides:
- Editorial appraisal
- Cover design
- Typesetting
- Printing
- Author promotion
- National book trade distribution, including sales, marketing and distribution through Macmillan Australia.

For details and inquiries, contact:
Brolga Publishing Pty Ltd
PO Box 12544
A'Beckett St VIC 8006

Phone: 03 9662 2633
Fax: 03 9671 4730
bepublished@brolgapublishing.com.au
markzocchi@brolgapublishing.com.au
ABN: 46 063 962 443